THE BIBLE
TELLS ME SO

THE BIBLE
TELLS ME SO

Volume I,
Studies in Abundant Living

Victor Paul Wierwille

American Christian Press
New Knoxville, Ohio 45871

Other books by Victor Paul Wierwille

Power for Abundant Living
Receiving The Holy Spirit Today
The New, Dynamic Church
    Volume II, Studies in Abundant Living
The Word's Way
    Volume III, Studies in Abundant Living
Are the Dead Alive Now?

Standard Book Number ISBN 0-910068-02-X
Library of Congress Catalog Card Number 70-176281
American Christian Press
New Knoxville, Ohio 45871
Published 1973
Printed in the United States of America

To my daughter
Mary Ellen Wierwille Somerville

Contents

Preface

The Bible Tells Me So is organized into four parts:
"Freedom From Bondage," "What We Believe = What
We Are," "Physical and Spiritual Wholeness" and
"The Word in Our Minds." Within each part are
chapters, each chapter having been researched and
originally written as an individual study. By loosely
grouping the studies into general topics, a person can
get a broader perspective as the parts fit together to
make up the larger whole.

However, because the chapters were written as
individual studies and then put into topical units,
occasionally a reader may find that all facets of the
topic are not covered; however, they have been
covered in other research writings. I know the con-
tents of Volume I of *Studies in Abundant Living* will
not only open up more of God's Word for you, but
will also uplift you – mentally and physically and
spiritually.

Let us put God's Word in our hearts and minds for
it alone can give us complete deliverance from the
darkness of this world.

Part I

Freedom

From Bondage

Part I

Freedom from Bondage

In order to live an abundant life, a person must first be free from mental bondage. The chains which bind one's mind are more painful and defeating than any other. As Christians, however, we have a personal liberator. Christ has delivered us. We must simply accept the freedom, once we know what He has done for us and how we are to go about receiving it.

"Release from Your Prisons" and "How to Avoid Being a Failure" tell us what has been done and how to receive the freedom which is ours. "Are You Limiting God" then focuses awareness on the truth that what God has promised He can give only if we allow. It is we who must appropriate the freedom from bondage which is available from God.

CHAPTER ONE

Release From Your Prisons

It is the absolute will of God for every person to be released from every prison or fetter which encases and binds. John 8 pointedly states God's will.

John 8:31,32 and 36:
... If ye continue in my word, *then* are ye my disciples indeed;

And ye shall know the truth, and the truth shall make you free.

If the Son therefore shall make you free, ye shall be free indeed.

These three short verses contain the key to release: we must believe the Word of God which is Truth and then we must know the Son who is the Way, the Truth and the Life. In following God's Word and in knowing His Son, we will not only be free, but we shall be free *indeed*.

3

God's will is for every one of us to be released today from whatever prison is holding us. Prisons are not only made of bars of steel. The prisons of our secret sins, things in our lives which we don't want to share with any other person in the world, are the most frustrating and defeating. The thoughts of self-condemnation that have been gnawing in the back of one's conscious and subconscious mind for years and years — thoughts of sickness and disease, fear, worry, anxiety, suicide, death — are the most tormenting and wretched kinds of prisons. It is not God's will for us to be so mentally bound; God's will is just the opposite as He has given total release from all negatives.

> Psalms 103:11,12:
> For as the heaven is high above the earth, *so* great is his mercy toward them that fear [respect] him.
>
> As far as the east is from the west, *so* far hath he removed our transgressions from us.

It is the will of God that all self-condemnation be gone because He wants to make us free indeed — not just half-free, but wholly-free persons.

Not only does God want us free of all the secret condemnation, but He wants us to be free from all

4

the powers of darkness in this world. He desires that we be free from resentments, from pride, from envyings, from jealousies, from obsessions and oppressions which have been eating away at us. He wants us to be released from these prisons, too.

Mankind has lived in the midst of evil ever since the devil received the power of this world.* Man has brought upon himself the evil with which he is surrounded. But, God so lovingly provided a way by which men might recognize and receive a greater and more wonderful power than they have ever known, that those who will to believe might be released from every prison enslaving their lives.

In Matthew 15:13 Jesus said, "Every plant, which my heavenly Father hath not planted, shall be rooted up." Every influence which is not based upon the accuracy of God's Word shall come to naught. Such influences lead only to imprisonment.

Hebrews 4:2:
For unto us was the gospel preached, as well as unto them: but the word preached did not profit them, not being mixed with faith [believing] in them that heard *it*.

*Luke 4:6: "And the devil said unto him, All this power will I give thee, and the glory of them: for that is delivered unto me; and to whomsoever I will I give it."

Freedom From Bondage

We must not only hear that Christ sets us free, we must believe and live accordingly.

A camera offers an appropriate analogy of the means by which you can get results to prayer and find release from your prisons. If you want an answer to prayer, first get your object in mind. You select what you want in your picture. This is step one: you're *clear* on what you want. Secondly, you use the range finder and focus the subject properly. Then consider the length of exposure of the picture so that all factors may work together for a perfect picture. After all of this, shoot the picture.

When you are focused on the picture of what you want, keep your mind stayed on it. If you allow something else to come in and take precedence over that picture you will get a blurred answer to prayer; you will not get the results you desire; you will not get release from the prison which is encasing you.*

If you want to get rid of something today, you must focus, dwell on what you want. It is the introduction of light that dispels darkness, not the dwelling on the darkness that introduces light. If you

_____

*James 1:6,7: "But let him ask in faith, nothing wavering. For he that wavereth is like a wave of the sea driven with the wind and tossed. For let not that man think that he shall receive any thing of the Lord."

6

want more business, better relations between employer and employee or a better job, get your desire in mind, focus on it and then determine the exposure time needed to accomplish the task.

If you want to get out of your prisons today, immediately change your thinking about your situation; change your subject of focus. As you change your thinking, you will draw a mental pattern for the things you *do* want in your life, which in turn will dispel and root out those things you do not want. You may say, "Well, that is not an easy thing to do, but I am going to try it. With God's help according to His Word, I am going to get out of this prison." However, if within half an hour you have forgotten to keep your thinking changed and you fall back into your old negative rut, you will be back living the same way you were before. Then don't wonder why you can't get an answer to prayer, why you cannot tap these resources, why the answer is not flowing as easily for you as it is for others, why you cannot have your release. The answer is that you only momentarily changed your mental image; you did not keep your picture in focus and allow proper exposure time.

The release from one's prisons depends upon two things: clearness and concern — the two "C's" of release. Get clear on what is wanted and then become concerned about receiving it. Get God's Word of deliverance and release into your mind and into your heart; eat it, drink it, sleep it and walk with it. Every time you take a step or every time you think about your situation or condition, thank God that the answer and your release is coming. Soon the negatives drop off and the positives become yours, the result of which is release from any prison you are in. It can be done; it will be done for as Philippians 4:13 says, "I can do all things through Christ which strengtheneth me."

How have you mentally pictured yourself for the past week, month, year, ten years? The picture that you carry of yourself with clearness and with concern is what you are. This law works for positive and negative thinking alike.

Most people believe that in order to gain the spiritual heights in life where they can tap the resources of God, it is necessary to strain and strive and struggle. They think that gaining spiritual results is like an air hammer — the harder one presses the hammer, the quicker he gets the job done. However, this is not the case. When we have stress and strain, we tie ourselves into knots. We will never get out of our prisons that way; just the opposite occurs — we bring more and more frustration to ourselves. It is not stress and strain, but believing and acting on The

8

Word that bring release.

> James 1:21:
> Wherefore lay apart all filthiness and superfluity of naughtiness, and receive with meekness the engrafted word, which is able to save your souls.

To "lay apart" means to "put off." We are to put off filthiness, the works of evil from the least to the worst form, and subjectively receive God's Word in the sense that we look to it and desire it because His Word is greater than we are. The "engrafted word" is the total implanted Word of God which He planted so close to us that we can absorb it until it becomes a part of us.

If we keep our minds renewed on God's Word, the love of God is perfected in our minds, and thus we give no opportunity to the flesh to hate (dislike) or slight a brother in Christ.

I John 2:11 says, "But he that hateth his brother is in darkness, and walketh in darkness, and knoweth not whither he goeth, because that darkness hath blinded his eyes." Absolute hate is possible only when someone is born of the seed of the devil, just as the *agapē* kind of love is possible only when a person is born of God's seed. The word "hate" may mean either "dislike" or "dislike issuing in the absolute

9

hate of the devil." In I John 2:11 "hate" is speaking of born-again believers hating, disliking, a brother.

He who slights or hates (dislikes) his brother has not renewed his mind on God's Word and is walking in darkness. Anyone walking in darkness just wanders aimlessly, not knowing where he is going. The Telegu translation of Proverbs 29:18 reads: "Where there is no knowledge of God the people wander aimlessly."

I do not care who you are or in what prison you may be, God will hear your prayer. Change yourself by changing your thinking patterns, and then the circumstances will change. Study God's Word and you will learn to know the Christ who has made you free. "If the Son therefore shall make you free, ye shall be free indeed." Outside of Christ we cannot be free. Jesus Christ was the liberator who set us free. He is the head of the Church.

The truth of The Word and of Christ is our light and power in life; this is our release from fears, worries, anxieties, frustrations, heartaches, headaches and everything else that comes along. This is our means to get out of the negative prisons of self-enslavement into the glorious liberty of children of God.

When you find yourself in one of life's prisons, get

a positive, clear picture of your freed self. Focus in on the positive image and thank God that right now you have the answer. Keep confessing and believing positively according to The Word, and your release will absolutely follow.

CHAPTER TWO

How To Avoid Being A Failure

The simplicity of the Word of God, the Bible, is astounding. Most of us have too much complicated theology and not enough simple believing. We are encased in so many negatives that even the positives are shrouded in darkness. We make God too difficult. Nobody wants to be a failure. God wants no failures — then, why be one? You don't have to be, if you don't want to. This is the exact meaning of this study.

Remember the story of the woman who lost one of the ten pieces of silver. Diligently she searched until she found it. After she came upon it, she called in all the neighbors and had a celebration because having lost a little piece of silver worth a few cents in United States currency, she finally found it. All the neighbors rejoiced with her. Can you imagine a little town in your section of the country getting excited over a few cents — let alone all the neighbors becoming so animated about it!

13

How did this woman avoid being a failure?

> Luke 15:8—10:
> Either what woman having ten pieces of silver, if she lose one piece, doth not light a candle, and sweep the house, and seek diligently till she find *it?*
>
> And when she hath found *it,* she calleth *her* friends and *her* neighbours together, saying, Rejoice with me; for I have found the piece which I had lost.
>
> Likewise, I say unto you, there is joy in the presence of the angels of God over one sinner that repenteth.

There are three interesting stories in the fifteenth chapter of Luke and all three deal with the same major subject. The first pertains to a shepherd having one hundred sheep, only ninety-nine of which were safe and sound. The third story is the one most people have erroneously called, "The Story of the Prodigal Son," more appropriately, "The Story of the Forgiving Father." The second is a story of a woman who avoided being a failure because she found one little piece of silver. You may laugh but it is true — her husband would have put her out of the house had she not found the lost piece of silver. Thus she would have been a failure as far as the whole town, including men and women, was concerned.

The pieces of silver are not merely ten ordinary pieces of money or ten coins with little significance; they are the most precious gift the bride receives from her bridegroom at the time of their marriage.

Each piece of silver is approximately the size of an American quarter. On one side of the piece of silver is engraved the insignia by which that particular family is known. If the family crest happened to be a sheep, well fed, protected and safe, that picture would be engraved on one side of all ten pieces of silver. On the other side would be stamped the year in which the piece of silver was made.

The husband gives this special dowry to his wife on their wedding day. As for dollars and cents, it isn't worth much, but the sentimental value is priceless. Money is no replacement for the lost piece of silver.

Both now and during the lifetime of Jesus, women in the Orient often receive lavish gifts of jewelry at the time of marriage. All the jewelry a woman receives becomes her own property and possession with the exception of the ten pieces of silver. She has all the legal rights to all her jewelry; the husband has

15

none. He cannot take her jewelry away under any circumstances, with one exception — the one jewel called "the ten pieces of silver." This jewel, in the event of the husband's death, must be handed back immediately to the husband's side of the family.

The jewel called the ten pieces of silver is worn by the wife only on very special occasions. Because of her love for her husband, she may put them on while her husband is away at work and gaze at herself in a mirror, appreciative of her husband's gift and love. Because they are so precious to her, she seldom wears them for fear of losing one. The twenty-fifth or fiftieth wedding anniversary would call for their wearing. Nothing less than the most special occasion.

When the wife does wear the ten pieces of silver jewelry, she wears five pieces of silver on one side of her head, towards the front of the head, and the other five pieces on the other side of her head. Each piece of silver has a little hook at the top. With these hooks the wife fastens the pieces of silver in her hair. Thus, you can understand how easily one piece, or a number of them, might become unhooked and, without her noticing it, she could lose them.

If she loses any of the pieces of silver, she will be put out of the house by her husband. The husband will not divorce her or be angry with her because of this, but simply expels the wife for she has disgraced him and his house and has brought reproach upon his family. The husband disposes of his spouse not because of the monetary value of the ten pieces of silver, but because losing one of the pieces of silver means the withdrawal of God's favor from the family. The loss of a piece of silver is looked upon as a curse on the whole family. Neither the husband nor the parents have spitefulness for her; but the wife will receive no sympathy from her husband, his parents or her other in-laws. A million dollars, given by the wife's family to the husband, would not rectify matters.

When the wife loses a piece of silver, the whole town is concerned about her for they know the consequences of being dishonored and expelled. The women of the entire city know what she must endure. Therefore, when the wife finds the lost piece of silver and knows that it is safe and secure, she calls in all her neighbors to rejoice with her over the piece of silver which she has found. She avoided being a failure.

We too can avoid being a failure by putting first things first.

Matthew 6:33:
But seek ye first the kingdom of God, and his

17

Freedom From Bondage

righteousness; and all these things shall be added unto you.

Seek anything else first and all things will be subtracted from you.

We are God's most precious creation. He wants no failures and He makes no failures. His will for us is success in everything.

The first step in this ladder of success is for a sinner to repent. Repentance is for unsaved sinners; confession is for saved sinners. God's love, the Father's heart, so yearns for the lost one that the Church will spend itself unreservedly, leaving nothing undone in order to find the one precious lost jewel. Who is that "jewel"? Each one of us is if we have not accepted Him.

You say, "What must I do?" The Father says, "Repent." How do you repent? Repentance is doing the will of God. It is not crying your eyes out, singing hymns or running to an altar. All these may or may not be involved, yet they are not repentance. Repentance is to do what God says; and He says in Romans 10:9, "That if thou shalt confess with thy mouth the Lord Jesus, and believe in thine heart that God hath raised him from the dead, thou shalt be saved." Repentance on your part is to confess with your

18

mouth the Lord Jesus as your personal Lord and Savior. It is to believe in your heart, your innermost being, that God has raised Jesus from the dead, that Jesus is resurrected and alive, yes, living *for* you and *in* you. That is repentance. It brings joy, not only to the angels in heaven, but also to the Father's heart for a most precious lost jewel has been found; one more life has avoided failure.

But you say, "Can I still do this? Can I rise up beyond all failure? Can I be sure?" Yes, you can be as sure as God Himself. For He stands behind His Word; He backs up His Word; He sees to it that His Word is performed.

In Him you are complete. You are a son of God; a joint-heir with Christ Jesus. You have resources unlimited. With Him you cannot fail, only succeed. Without Him, you cannot succeed, only fail. His invitation is to you, for it is to all, "Come unto me ... and I will give you rest." "... Lo, I am with you always ...." "... I will never leave thee, nor forsake thee." Come! Avoid being a failure!

* * *

You are the one to now decide
Whether to believe Him or toss Him aside.

19

Freedom From Bondage

You are the one to make up your mind,
Whether to accept Him or linger behind.
Take Him or leave Him, which will you do,
Believing is assurance of no failure for you.

CHAPTER THREE

Are You Limiting God?

Jesus Christ is the sweetest name I know, for it is in His name, and His name alone, that I see the unlimited possibilities in man. It is in the name of Jesus Christ that men and women are saved, born again, converted. It is in the name of Jesus Christ that the sick are healed to rise up again and declare the glory of the Lord. It is in the name of Jesus Christ that devil spirits are cast out and people are forever freed in body and mind. Unless we know that name of Jesus Christ as a vital living reality in our lives, we are most definitely limiting God.

The spirit of God is born within us the very moment we accept and believe on the Lord Jesus Christ and that God raised Him from the dead. This is a supernatural miracle of God. We have nothing to do with this new birth except to allow it to take place in our lives. God is the miracle worker. He is the one who creates a new spirit within us and makes us His children. From then on, we are God's children, we

21

belong to the family of God, we are children of God, sons of God, and joint-heirs with Christ Jesus. Then we are no longer servants who know not what their Master is about to do, but we are sons, sons of God. Satan then has no further legal rights over us unless we permit him to usurp authority which he does not rightfully possess. We may limit God in our lives by not knowing what is legally ours as sons of God by Christ Jesus.

When Christ died on Calvary, He was our complete substitute for sin and the consequences of sin. Nothing was left undone in His substitution for us. When we begin to see this truth and we accept the work Christ accomplished as a finished reality, we become spirit-filled men and women who are well-pleasing in God's sight.

When this great transformation takes place and we do not limit God, then we will not talk about worry, fear, anxiety, sickness and want. We forget those negatives for we are sons by the One who overcame. We are men and women who refuse to limit the power of God in us because we desire to bring to the world the knowledge of the living Christ. When we do not limit God, we will be living in The Word and The Word will be living in us. Our life will be the story of the vine and the branches.

II Corinthians 9:8:
And God *is* able to make all grace abound
toward you; that ye, always having all sufficiency in all *things* may abound to every good
work.

Have we been limiting God in our lives? We must
be if we do not have all sufficiency in everything.
Sufficiency is the will of God for His children in
order that His children may abound unto every good
work. Our having sufficiency is God's will for us; yet
how many of us have limited God by not allowing
Him to fulfill this promise in our lives? How slow we
have been to realize that God is our ability, that He is
the life of our lives, the strength of our strength, that
He is our sufficiency.

We frequently limit God in ourselves by our wrong
believing, by accepting the knowledge that comes to
us through our senses. Our reason says, "That just
cannot be," and so we confess the negative, when all
the time His spirit within us is crying out, "Sufficiency in everything." We have been so schooled to
revere the knowledge that comes to us through our
five senses that we fail to recognize the knowledge
that comes from the higher realm, the spiritual, where
the Word of God, and not reason, has first place.
Both realms or worlds are here: the natural world is
factual; the spiritual world is true. As there are four

kingdoms in this world, and one supersedes the other: the plant kingdom, animal kingdom, kingdom of man and the Kingdom of God; so, there is a natural world and a supernatural or spiritual world. The natural world and everything in it comes to the mind through or by way of the natural senses. The truths of the spiritual world are absolutely *not* dependent upon the senses, but rather on the spirit from God in man.

We cannot know anything about the spiritual world by way of the senses. That is why Paul said by divine inspiration in I Corinthians 2:14, "But the natural man receiveth not the things of the Spirit of God: for they are foolishness unto him ... because they [spiritual matters] are spiritually discerned."

Spiritual things from the spiritual world may be known in this world only by the spirit which dwells in us. Then, and only then, can the Spirit relate impressions and truths to us about the spiritual world and make them logical. Then, and only then, do we have the God-given ability within us, making known to us things about the spiritual world.

Time and time again, after I have explained the difference between the natural and spiritual worlds, how the one supersedes the other and that two entirely different sets of laws are in existence, people have said to me that they were thereafter able to give

God the place He deserves. Then they refused to limit God within themselves.

Few people realize the great spiritual truth of Christ's substitution and the believer's righteousness. A man in whom the new creation lives is righteous before God, according to the Word of God. The born-again man is righteous, and to be righteous means that we can stand before God in the righteousness with which He clothed us by our acceptance of Christ as our substitute for sin and the consequences of sin.

I will give you a definition of righteousness that will help you to break the powers of darkness in and over your life. Righteousness is your God-given ability to stand in the Father's presence without a sense of sin, guilt or condemnation. That means that you as a child of God can also stand in the very presence of Satan without fear or defeat because you know your rights in Christ and you have refused to limit God in you.

When we recognize that God in Christ lives in us, that kind of believing makes us victorious over Satan in every way. We then come to the place where we rely upon the power or the ability of God in Christ in us. We recognize our place in life and we work knowing that God in Christ in us assures us of success. We go to our shops with natural confidence — into our homes, into our businesses, knowing that God in Christ in us makes a winning combination in every situation.

I want you to notice Ephesians 3:20. As a matter of fact, I want you to learn it so well that it will be a living reality in you day by day for then I know you will have released the power of God in your life.

> Ephesians 3:20:
> Now unto him that is able to do exceeding abundantly above all that we ask or think, according to the power [or ability of God] that worketh in us.

How much are we allowing God to work in us? That is the paramount question. It is not a question of God's willingness or ability. It is simply a question of allowing the limitlessness of God to live in us and work in us, to will and to do His good pleasure. He will do exceeding abundantly above all that we ask or think, but only to the degree that we manifest the internal potential power.

> I John 4:4:
> Ye are of God ... because greater is he that is in you, than he that is in the world.

Thus, I know that the "more abundant life" which is spoken of in John 10:10 is in me. He is no longer *with* me to convict me of my sin and shortcomings; but He is *in* me to guide me and lead me into all truth and reality. Now we are "labourers together with God ...." Now we are God's fellow-workers. What a glorious privilege.

Are you limiting God? Why not release the power of God that is latent within you, and believe God for the abundance which He has promised?

Part II

What We Believe

Equals

What We Are

Part II

What We Believe = What We Are

The law of believing is dynamically powerful, yet so simple. The law, simply stated, is that what we believe for or expect, we get. This applies in every realm: physical, mental, material, spiritual. Thus it is this law which basically controls the abundant life. Only if we believe and expect abundance will we ever realize abundance in our lives.

"The Synchronized Life" shows that our lives are molded by our believing — both by positive and negative believing. This law is further explained and proved in "The Law of Believing" so that we will become aware of our own thinking and then be able to control our thinking so as to manifest the abundant life which is promised in God's Word.

CHAPTER FOUR

The Synchronized Life

Whatever a person believes is directly reflected in what he confesses. What a person confesses in his innermost being is what he brings into manifestation in his life. If a person goes through life confessing that he has great need, he will definitely have great need. If he confesses sickness, he will continue to be sick and afflicted because of the law that what one believes in the depth of his soul absolutely appears in his life.

The "synchronized life" is simply stated by this formula: confession of belief yields receipt of confession. If you will confess with your mouth at the same time that you confess in your heart what The Word says, you will have power. Your prayers will be answered as you apply these keys in your life by your action. Thus, the abundant resources of heaven are made available to you. But, likewise, if you simultaneously confess with your mouth and heart the negatives of this world, you will manifest these

31

What We Believe = What We Are

crippling negatives.

If you confess Christ as the Lord in your life, your confession is a reality to you. In your heart you know He is Lord because you believed God has raised Him from the dead. When you confess that you are a new creature in Christ, old things pass away and all things become new according to your confession. If you confess that you are a son of God and the Bible says that you are a son, then you are a son of God. If your confession is that you are an heir of the Father, then everything that the Father has becomes yours because you are confessing exactly what The Word says.

The Word declares that the devil both *was* and *is* defeated. It stipulates he has no legal rights over the Christian. If Satan has no power over the Christian, why do you want to confess that he has power over you? Every time you make a negative confession you are contradicting God's Word. If the devil's power is defeated, as it is, then his power cannot touch you when you believe The Word. But, you must *confess* that you know the power of God in your life. You must confess what God says in His Word and then The Word becomes a reality in your life. Whenever you dare to confess that you are what The Word says you are and act on what The Word teaches, you will find that your prayers are answered.

So long as I cannot get my mouth and my heart coordinated on some point that is confirmed by The Word, I have no power with God. When I confess that God does not answer my prayer, that He does not like me, that I have a sickness because God gave it to me, or that I am bound by something evil because it is God's will for me to be thus disciplined in life, or that I must suffer for the glory of God — then I am not saying what The Word says and I will bring into evidence in my life the result of my confession.

Psalms 18 contains a beautiful simile which illustrates how we are to get our mind and actions coordinated.

> Psalms 18:33:
> He maketh my feet like hinds' *feet,* and setteth me upon my high places.

A hind is a mother deer, one of the most sure-footed animals in the world. When she goes up the side of a mountain with her young following her, she takes her back feet and places them exactly where her front feet were first placed to test for loose stones on the slope. If she did not test that rocky incline with her front feet, the loose stones would cause her to slip and fall down into the ravine below. This exact tracking means life both to the hind and to her young.

What We Believe = What We Are

"He maketh my feet like hinds' feet." He maketh them. That is, He makes it so that I may learn to walk by The Word so that my "hind feet" will track with my "front feet (representing The Word)." Thus, where The Word has set its feet, there also will I put my feet.

If you stand upon the Word of God and you confess that Word, you become what the Word of God says. This is the synchronized life.

Romans tells us how dear and how powerful God's children are.

> Romans 8:35–37:
> Who shall separate us from the love of Christ? *shall* tribulation, or distress, or persecution, or famine, or nakedness, or peril, or sword?
>
> As it is written, For thy sake we are killed all the day long; we are accounted as sheep for the slaughter.
>
> Nay, in all these things we are more than conquerors through him that loved us.

I am not just saying this; *God* said it. Do you believe God's Word? He said you are *more* than a conqueror through Him who loved you.

34

Romans 8:38,39:
For I am persuaded, that neither death, nor life, nor angels, nor principalities, nor powers, nor things present, nor things to come,

Nor height, nor depth, nor any other creature, shall be able to separate us from the love of God, which is in Christ Jesus our Lord.

This is the declared, confirmed Word of God. When you begin to confess that Word, it becomes a reality in your life. Until that time you will be defeated by satanic principalities and powers on every hand because of your confession. Know The Word, confess The Word and act upon The Word. That is what is meant by a synchronized life.

Determine now that you will never again make a negative confession. Learn what and how to confess. Confess from the heart, with your mouth, what has been confirmed by The Word. Confess what the Bible says you are, not what you think you are, not what your next door neighbor says you are, not what your best friend may say you are. Hold fast to what The Word says.

We have been delivered from the power of darkness: Satan, evil and wrong.

Colossians 1:13:
Who hath delivered us from the power of darkness, and hath translated *us* into the kingdom of
[by] his dear Son.*

The next time evil or negatives come into your
mind, immediately declare The Word and say, "I
confess that I have been delivered from the power of
darkness by my Lord and Savior, Jesus Christ." Keep
saying this and soon it will be a reality in your life. If
you have been translated into the Kingdom of God
by the work of His dear Son, then you are not in the
kingdom of the devil. Do you think you can be in the
Kingdom of God and of the devil at the same time?
He has delivered us from the power of evil and we
are in the Kingdom of God.

People think they must strive to become good
before God will bless them. I assure you that God will
never bless you because of your goodness, but rather
because of your believing. How do you get rid of
darkness in a room? The darkness is gone as quickly
as the light comes. So when we allow the light of The
Word to come into our lives, the darkness is dispelled.
There is nothing in The Word that says anything
about our feelings, it says *believe.* All that God has

*The literal translation according to usage is: "Who hath rescued us
out from among the exercise or operative influence of darkness (kingdom) and separated us, bringing us as citizens into His kingdom by the
work of His dear Son."

given comes to you by believing without respect to how good or how bad you are. That is love. That is what Christ came to bring.

As we act on the promises of God, they become real to us and are evidenced in our lives. Synchronize your believing and confession on the promises of God's Word and you will manifest a more than abundant life in Christ Jesus.

CHAPTER FIVE

The Law of Believing

I know that the abundant life is available today to those who understand and apply the law of believing.

Regarding this subject, I want to call your attention to Mark 9. This is a rather long story; but if I am to teach you the law of believing, you must get the truth of this record into your heart and life.

Mark 9:14—27:
And when he came to *his* disciples, he saw a great multitude about them, and the scribes questioning with them.

And straightway all the people, when they beheld him, were greatly amazed, and running to *him* saluted him.

And he asked the scribes, What question ye with them?

And one of the multitude answered and said, Master, I have brought unto thee my son, which hath a dumb spirit;

And wheresoever he taketh him, he teareth him: and he foameth, and gnasheth with his teeth, and pineth away: and I spake to thy disciples that they should cast him out; and they could not.

He answereth him, and saith, O faithless generation, how long shall I be with you? how long shall I suffer you? bring him unto me.

And they brought him unto him: and when he saw him, straightway the spirit tare him; and he fell on the ground, and wallowed foaming.

And he asked his father, How long is it ago since this came unto him? And he said, Of a child.

And ofttimes it hath cast him into the fire, and into the waters, to destroy him: but if thou canst do anything, have compassion on us, and help us.

Jesus said unto him, If thou canst believe, all things *are* possible to him that believeth.

And straightway the father of the child cried out, and said with tears, Lord, I believe; help thou mine unbelief.

When Jesus saw that the people came running together, he rebuked the foul spirit, saying unto him, *Thou* dumb and deaf spirit, I charge thee, come out of him, and enter no more into him.

And *the spirit* cried, and rent him sore, and came out of him: and he was as one dead; insomuch that many said, He is dead.

But Jesus took him by the hand, and lifted him up; and he arose.

The man brought his son for healing. He reported to Jesus that the disciples could not remedy the situation. The disciples must have felt stupid for this was a public demonstration and nobody in private, let alone in public, wants to look like a fool. These were the same disciples who had before had great victory and success in healing the sick. Now they had come to an impasse. What stymied them?

Jesus perceived the trouble immediately when the father said, "If thou canst do anything, have compassion on us, and help us." Jesus took that "if" which the father had directed at the disciples first and

41

next at Jesus, and gave it back to the father where it belonged. "Jesus said unto him, If thou canst believe, all things are possible to him that believeth." Many people like to lay the blame for their unbelief and inability to receive on someone else. The disciples were victims of the blame in this situation. The disciples, were caught in this man's trap, but not Jesus. Many people would like for others to do their believing for them; they just do not want to learn how to believe for themselves. Many times people simply do not know how to believe. Jesus understood the situation clearly and He said to the father of the child, "If you can believe. I know that my disciples believe, and the fact that they could not remove the cause is not their fault. They could believe until Doom's Day for your child without any result; but if *you* can believe, then something will happen."

Wherever possible, Jesus always demanded believing. When we study the miracles of healing, we find that Jesus required the believing of the parents for the healing of their children. For example, in Matthew 15:22 we see that the Canaanite woman had great believing for the healing of her daughter who was vexed with a devil.

In the case of demented persons, who are mentally incapable, believing was not required. The following are examples of such cases: Mark 1:23ff and

Luke 4:33ff; Matthew 8:16ff; Mark 1:32ff; Luke 4:41; Matthew 8:28ff; Luke 8:26ff; Mark 5:1ff; Matthew 9:32; and Acts 16:16.

In the case of raising the dead, as recorded in Mark 5:35ff and Luke 8:49ff, we read that Jesus told the father of the dead child, "Be not afraid, only believe." When Jesus raised Lazarus from the dead, the passage does not say that anyone believed except Jesus. In Acts 9:36ff, where Peter raised Dorcas from the dead, he put everyone out of the room and then prayed and commanded her to arise.

In every Biblical record believing is always required on the part of everyone having a need, with the exceptions indicated above: certain types of mental derangement, dead people and children.

There is power in believing. There is power in this world to which you and I as born-again believers have easy access. This power will enable us to overcome our shortcomings and our difficulties, bringing release and victory to our lives. This power is from God. He is everywhere present, which means that He is with you right now. The key involved is knowing and receiving His power, which is the basis on which the whole abundant life hinges. The law of believing brings phenomenal results to all those who apply and practice the principles.

You may believe rightly or wrongly. Believing works both ways, and you bring to yourself whatever you believe. Matthew 9 and Job 3 show the types of believing and their results.

> Matthew 9:20–22:
> And, behold, a woman, which was diseased with an issue of blood twelve years came behind *him* and touched the hem of his garment:
>
> For she said within herself, If I may but touch his garment, I shall be whole.
>
> But Jesus turned him about, and when he saw her, he said, Daughter, be of good comfort; thy faith [believing] hath made thee whole.
>
> Job 3:25:
> For the thing which I greatly feared [believed] is come upon me, and that which I was afraid of is come unto me.

Fear, worry and anxiety are types of believing. If you worry, have fear and are anxious you will receive the fruit of your negative believing which is defeat.

The law of believing works equally effectively for both the sinner and the saint; however, the believer, because of the spirit from God within him, may bring forth more abundantly. If you doubt your recovery from sickness, you will by all means slow up and retard your own progress. Right believing is constantly knowing God's power and presence are in you and with you in every situation! How you think about the problem with which you are confronted at this very moment will determine the outcome. If you doubt its success, you have, by your own believing, determined its unsuccessful outcome. Apply the positive method of the law of believing to every situation in life, to every problem that comes your way, for "... if thou canst believe, all things *are* possible to him that believeth."

Saying some formal prayer will never release you and bring positive results to your life. You cannot hope, think or guess at this game of living. You just believe that God is in you and that He is with you always, even unto the end of this age.

I John 4:4:
... greater is he that is in you, then he that is in the world.

The evil of the world can never make you do evil or wrong unless you permit it through your own weakness of character or lack of believing.

45

Once you start practicing the law of believing —
right believing, believing God — you will find that
the evil things that have been governing your life will
soon fade away. God is always the victor over evil;
but it is up to you to believe God and to make His
will your will.

In all the New Testament epistles, you will never
find Christian believers urged to have faith; they
already have faith as believers, and they are en-
couraged to believe God and express what they
already have.

> Romans 12:3:
> ... according as God hath dealt to every man the
> measure of faith.

The word "believe" is a verb which connotes
action. Therefore, believing the Word of God, taking
the Word of God literally and acting upon it, brings
results. This is the law of believing and this is the
action that will bring release and victory to your life
in every situation. "If thou canst believe, all things
are possible [presently available] to him that believeth."

46

Part III

Physical and Spiritual Wholeness

Part III

Physical and Spiritual Wholeness

The Bible clearly tells us that, as Christians, God has richly provided for us. Since God has given us His abundance, in all fairness we should accept "The Counsel of the Lord." He, only, is wise, undeceived and worthy of following

"God Rescued Us" and separated us from the unbelievers when we didn't even know we needed rescuing. God, when we believed on His Son, snatched us from Satan's influence and gave us citizenship in His Kingdom.

"You Are Righteous Now" assures us that God through Jesus Christ has made us acceptable in His sight. Our spiritual worthiness is established beyond a shadow of doubt.

"The Broken Body and the Shed Blood" is a marvelous truth about the significance of the communion observance. The cup and the bread of communion not only signifies spiritual harmony with God, but indicates physical wholeness as well. This truth is so powerful and helpful, yet virtually unknown and unpracticed.

"Complete in Him" is a bird's-eye view of our completeness in every way in Christ. God by His Son Jesus Christ has totally provided for all our needs. He has outfitted us in His completeness.

CHAPTER SIX

The Counsel of the Lord

The Old Testament speaks of the Lord's counsel.

Proverbs 19:21:
There are many devices in a man's heart; nevertheless the counsel of the Lord, that shall stand.

Jeremiah 10:23:
O Lord, I know that the way of man *is* not in himself: *it is* not in man that walketh to direct his steps.

Proverbs 16:9:
A man's heart deviseth his way: but the Lord directeth his steps.

How desperately revealing these truths are! A man in his heart thinks many things yet all the plans of a man's heart are worthless. It is only the Lord who can truly direct a man's steps, and it is only the counsel of the Lord, the Word of God, that shall stand.

Physical and Spiritual Wholeness

How these men of God of old laid bare the natural man's heart and how bare and impotent is the carnal Christian to direct his own life! We need the Lord to direct our steps according to the revealed Word of God. Of a necessity the internal anxiety and hostility of the natural man is raised and even the thoughts of the carnal Christian are roused to indignation to learn these truths for they are very humbling. It is the very last thing the natural man or the carnal Christian wants to admit, for each man thinks he is right in his own eyes and each man thinks he can direct his own way. If you will notice the prayer life of most Christians, you will see that they try to direct the Lord as to what He ought to do. They even imply that if man had the direction of the affairs of the world and of the Church, he would soon have things very different from what they are, and the Kingdom of God would come to pass upon the earth in spite of or without God. The carnal Christian needs to humble himself before the Lord Almighty. The old nature, even in the child of God, is not easily overcome; but the Lord alone brings us to the realization of knowing, "I am astray, save me. I am empty, fill me. I am ignorant, teach me. I am perplexed, counsel me. I am weak, strengthen me. I am deceived, deliver me."

The one great work of the Spirit is to direct the heart. Man's work always begins at the wrong end to accomplish things. Man always begins on the outside hoping to work toward the inside; man cleanses the outside of the pitcher while the uncleanness remains within. Man's aim is always to reform life; so he sweeps, garnishes and polishes it. This is the way of religion frequently called Christianity. But this is truly not Christianity for Christianity is not what man does; Christianity is what God has done through Christ. The object of religion will always be to direct the flesh, and by rules and regulations try to make the flesh bring forth spiritual fruit. All man's effort is in vain because it is man's heart that is at fault.

> Matthew 15·11,19,20:
> Not that which goeth into the mouth defileth a man; but that which cometh out of the mouth, this defileth a man.
>
> For out of the heart proceed evil thoughts, murders, adulteries, fornications, thefts, false witness, blasphemies:
>
> These are *the things* which defile a man: but to eat with unwashen hands defileth not a man.

Man consistently endeavors to direct his own way, and for the most part he does his best to direct the ways of all others. Religion is made up of ordinances for the flesh like "touch not, taste not; handle not ...," which are nothing more or less than "... commandments and doctrines of men," as Colossians 2:21 and 22 tell.

How truly opposite is the working of the Holy Spirit. All man's forms of godliness are simply the doctrines and commandments of men which begin with the flesh and continue in fleshly corruption ending in death. But the Holy Spirit makes known unto us through The Word the condition of ourselves. The Holy Spirit shows us our sins and follies, our frailties and our infirmities, our weaknesses and our errors, our faults and our failings. The wisdom of Christ in doing His Father's will rules our walk, and the spirit with which we are filled — that power from on high which energizes us — will bring forth newness of life.

The Word of God directs the renewed-mind Christian to the work of Christ — a work begun in grace, which continues in grace in this life and terminates with Christ in His glory. Our completeness in Christ in our renewed mind is the measure to which we will manifest the power of the gift of holy spirit.

One of the big questions always is: Do our works glorify Him? Those who are walking in the spirit will constantly keep glorifying God with their actions, while man's works will ever turn our thoughts to man and direct our attention to man's walk or to man's acts or to man's experiences. Man's work is always the end for those who glory in themselves. It is the spirit's work *which glorifies God and enables man to do God's work.

The question we must continue to ask ourselves day by day is: Does our walk glorify God? This is the one and only test we may apply. This test tells us whether our walk is under the direction of the Lord or whether we are simply acting by our self-centered senses, diverted from God's Spirit by another spirit. The church in Corinth was specifically warned against "another spirit," namely, a different spirit which they had not received according to II Corinthians 11:4. This tells us that there is specifically another spirit who is at work to misdirect and to deceive. This spirit from Satan would try to control and deceive us today, even as II Corinthians 11:3 says, "... as the serpent beguiled Eve through his subtilty."

When we are under the influence of "another spirit," we can be ever so "religious" while totally out of alignment and harmony with God. One spirit is from the God and Father of our Lord Jesus Christ. The other spirit is from the god of this world, who is the devil. So many things are said and done as the work of the Holy Spirit of God which are wholly

*Philippians 2:13: "For it is God which worketh in you [by way of the gift in you] both to will and to do of *his* good pleasure.

53

different from anything recorded in the Word of God, and yet religion maintains that they are truth. In reality there is only confusion, and "God is not the author of confusion," as I Corinthians 14:33 says. So then, whether enemies abound, Satan assaults, days be dark with doubts and fears increasing, even then we are "more than conquerors" through Him who loved us and gave Himself for us. It is the Lord God who must direct our hearts unto His love to the end that we will make the same confession as recorded in Psalms.

Psalms 73:22–25:
So foolish *was* I, and ignorant: I was *as* a beast before thee.

Nevertheless I *am* continually with thee: thou hast holden *me* by my right hand.

Thou shalt guide me with thy counsel, and afterward receive me *to* glory.

Whom have I in heaven *but thee?* and *there is* none upon earth *that* I desire beside thee.

CHAPTER SEVEN

God Rescued Us

In order to understand that God rescued us, we first should know how we got in a position to need rescuing. The roots of mankind's dilemma stem back to the time of Genesis 1:28 when God originally gave man rulership, dominion and authority over this world. Man was placed in this world as the ruler and caretaker. But when sin entered the earthly realm, due to man's disobedience to God, man lost his authority, dominion, rulership. The devil, who was handed the rulership in man's fall, offered to give it to Jesus Christ in the temptation as recorded in Luke 4.

The devil said to Jesus Christ in Luke 4:6, "... for that [power and glory of the kingdoms of this world] is delivered unto me." Therefore, unto this very day the world in which you and I live is Satan's realm. We live in the realm which is under Satan's rulership. According to Ephesians 2:1 all people are born in this world "... dead in trespasses and sins" and (verse 12)

55

"... having no hope, and without God ...." Being in such a dire state, we definitely needed rescuing.

> Colossians 1:13:
> Who hath delivered us from the power of darkness, and hath translated *us* into the kingdom of [by] his dear Son.

The word "delivered" is more emphatically translated "rescued." God in Christ "rescued us." Notice that this verb is in the past tense. Therefore, God no longer needs to rescue us; He has already done so. The word "from" is the Greek word *ek* meaning "out of" or "out from the center" (as of a circle). What did He rescue us out of or out from among? "The power of darkness."

This world, which is darkness and is under the dominion of the devil, is that which God has rescued us out from among. He rescued us out of this world even while we are still dwelling here. That God could do this is one of the greatest of miracles.

The word "power" in the above verse ("from the power of darkness") is the Greek word *exousia* from which English derives the word "exercise." He has delivered us from the exercised power of darkness, the exercising influence of this kingdom of darkness.

56

The word "translated" ("translated *us* into the kingdom of his dear Son") in Sanskrit is "citizenship." He rescued us out from among the exercised power of darkness and gave us citizenship. This is a tremendous truth.

What does this citizenship in His kingdom entail? To begin, let us look at the Greek word for "city," *polis.* The cities in Biblical times were surrounded by walls. The wall policed the city. The walled city was the *polis.* The people within the walls were called the people of the *polis.* The walls guarded them from being attacked. Walls were never built to keep people *inside* the city but to keep the enemy *out.* The walls formed a protection, not to keep the free people of a city or a state enclosed, but to keep the enemy away from the free people. A free citizen in a city is called a *politēs,* from which we get the word "politics." Biblically speaking, we are citizens of a kingdom — we are politicians.

Abraham searched for a city, *polis.*

Hebrews 11:9,10:
By faith he [Abraham] sojourned in the land of promise, as *in* a strange country, dwelling in tabernacles with Isaac and Jacob, the heirs with him of the same promise:
For he [Abraham] looked [already] for a city

[*polis*] which hath foundations, whose builder and maker *is* God.

Abraham in his day looked forward to a city, not here upon earth, but a *polis* "... whose builder and maker *is* God." This city is protected with the hedge of God wherein the people would be free citizens.

An example of *politeia*, a derivative of *polis*, is found in Ephesians.

Ephesians 2:12:
That at that time ye were without Christ, being aliens from the commonwealth [community, *politeia*] of Israel, and strangers from the covenants of promise, having no hope, and without God in the world.

At the time referred to in Ephesians 2, Israel had forsaken God and so God was not able to bless them. Because they had walked away from Him, they no longer had freedom and protection where they dwelled. They were in bondage.

Politeuma, from the root word *polis,* is used in Philippians where it is strangely translated "conversation."

Philippians 3:20:
For our conversation [*politeuma,* citizenship] is

in heaven; from whence also we look for the Saviour, the Lord Jesus Christ.

Our citizenship, our free life, is in heaven. Even while we are yet on this earth, we have the promise of being citizens in a free state.

Hebrews 13:14:
For here [on this earth] have we no continuing city [*polis*], but we seek one to come.

If we have no continuing city here, we can never have complete freedom; therefore, "... we seek one to come." That city which is to come must be uncorrupted inside and protected all around to insure the citizens of total freedom. This city could only be the city whose builder and maker is God.

Now we look for the continuing city; but what about our life before we were delivered from the power of darkness? Ephesians tells us of our former citizenship.

Ephesians 2:3:
Among whom also we all had our conversation [life of negative conduct] in times past in the lusts of our flesh, fulfilling the desires of the flesh and of the mind; and were by nature the children of wrath, even as others.

By the very event of being born into this world, we were children of whose realm? Satan's. This is the meaning of the word "wrath" in "children of wrath." We were born children of Satan's realm — not spiritually, but physically. Physically I was born a child under Satan's rulership, dead in trespasses and sins without God and without hope in this world. But God changed all this, as recorded in Ephesians 2.

Ephesians 2:4—6:
But God, who is rich in mercy, for his great love wherewith he loved us,

Even when we were dead in [full of] sins, hath quickened us together with Christ, (by grace ye are saved;)

And hath raised [past tense] *us* up together [with Christ], and made *us* sit together in heavenly *places* [the text gives "in the heavenlies"] in Christ Jesus.

Who did the quickening; who raised us up; who made us sit in the heavenlies? God.

Verses 7—9:
That in the ages to come he might shew the exceeding riches of his grace in *his* kindness

toward us through Christ Jesus.

For by grace are ye saved through faith; and that not of yourselves: *it is* the gift of God:

Not of works, lest any man should boast.

When we were born in this world, we were alive physically yet dead spiritually, "without God and without hope." Something had to happen to us. God, who is rich in mercy and grace, saved us.

Verse 10:
For we are his workmanship, created in Christ Jesus unto good works, which God hath before ordained that we should walk in them.

If God saved us, then we are not our own workmanship; we are sons, *His* workmanship. God's workmanship came to bear when we were spiritually dead; at that time God made us alive.

Colossians 2:13:
And you, being dead in your sins and the uncircumcision of your flesh, hath he quickened [made alive] together with him [Christ], having forgiven you all trespasses.

God created us in Christ Jesus and graciously

pardoned our sins. But before God could make us
alive, He had to have us as "raw material" to work
on. Thus, the question becomes: How does He create
us in Christ Jesus?

> John 6:44:
> No man can come to me, except the Father
> which hath sent me draw him ....

We can be made alive, we can obtain this citizenship, only if the Father does the drawing. We cannot
raise ourselves by our own bootstraps; we cannot save
ourselves. No man, not one person, can come to
Christ and be saved except the Father draws him. To
receive eternal life a man must be drawn by God
away from the clutches and rulership of Satan. Jesus
used the word "draw" again in John.

> John 12:32:
> And I, if I be lifted up from the earth, will draw
> all *men* unto me.

Jesus said in John 6:44 that only the Father can do
the drawing; yet here it says that Christ is going to do
the drawing. What is the answer? Into the world ruled
by Satan in which you and I live, there came a person
who was conceived by the Holy Spirit and born of
Mary. This person came into the devil's world having
no darkness in Him for He was the light of the world.

He knew no sin. He became sin so that you and I might become the righteousness of God in Him. Furthermore, He was in this world, but He was not of — He did not belong to — this world. When Christ was in the world the Scripture says that God was at work in Him.

II Corinthians 5:19:
... God was in Christ, reconciling the world [the people in it] unto himself ....

God actually *draws* through the death and resurrection of Jesus Christ who, according to Isaiah 53:6, carried "the iniquity of us all." Because of Jesus Christ's death, God could then draw or rescue the believers from the rulership of Satan and give them citizenship in His kingdom.

Before God rescued us, we were dead in sins. But God sent His only-begotten Son who was the means by which we could be rescued. We are God's workmanship created through the accomplishments of Christ Jesus. God rescued us.

John 3:16:
For God so loved the world, that he gave his only begotten Son ....

God sent His Son, who had no darkness and

no sin, and drew His Son unto Himself. Because of Jesus' death and resurrection God draws us. He made possible our great hope of glory: "... Christ in you, the hope of glory." God rescued us out of this realm of Satan and gave us citizenship in His kingdom.

> Colossians 1:13:
> Who hath delivered us from the power of darkness, and hath translated *us* into the kingdom of [by] his dear Son.

This kingdom cannot be the "kingdom of his dear Son" for the Son has no kingdom of His own; the "kingdom" is the kingdom of God. The word "of" should be "by." It is the genitive of origin. God rescued us out of the exercised power of the kingdom of darkness, the rulership of Satan, and gave us citizenship in His kingdom by what His Son Jesus Christ did for us here upon earth.

> Galatians 1:4:
> Who gave himself for our sins, that he might deliver us [rescue us] from [out from among] this present evil world, according to the will of God and our Father.

Until we are born again, we are children of wrath; we are in a physical world which belongs to the devil; it is his kingdom. When we are born again, we become

"... blameless and harmless, the sons of God, without rebuke [from God], in the midst of a crooked and perverse nation [kingdom,]" according to Philippians 2:15.

God drew us and rescued us out from among the exercised influences of Satan. There are people, however, in Satan's world who will never be saved for they refuse to believe. But, for those of us who want to believe, God by His foreknowledge has rescued us out from the power of Satan. When God separated us and rescued us, He brought us as citizens into His kingdom by the efforts of His dear Son.

It was God who sent His only-begotten Son into the world to seek and to save those who are lost, specifically those of us who desire to be saved. God rescued us even while we are still living in this world.

Already we have citizenship in God's kingdom He has already "... made *us* sit together in heavenly *places* in Christ Jesus," as told in Ephesians 2:6. Legally speaking, in Christ we were circumcised with His circumcision. When Christ died, we died with Him. When He was buried, we were buried in the baptism of His burial. When He arose, we arose with Him. When He ascended, we ascended with Him. When Christ conquered, we conquered with Him. When He was seated, we were seated with Him. When

Physical and Spiritual Wholeness

He lead "captivity captive" and "gave gifts unto men," we were given the power to live victoriously even in the realm of Satan, having the ability to manifest the power of God in the more abundant life. What a revelation to the soul of man! What glory, what joy, what peace, what bliss! We are rescued now.

You Are Righteous Now

Many born-again believers are spiritually defeated in this life because of sin-consciousness. They have been saved, but Satan comes to their minds and tells them they are not good enough for salvation because of the many years they lived in sin. This spiritual antagonism and defeat comes when a person does not realize what has been given to him by Jesus Christ. When a person becomes a Christian, he is legally made righteous in Christ.

What is righteousness? Righteousness is the God-given justification whereby a person stands in the presence of God without any consciousness of sin, guilt or shortcomings.* Righteousness is some-

*Romans 8:33 says, "Who shall lay any thing to the charge of God's elect? *It is* God that justifieth."

thing God imparts; it is something God gave to you when you were born again, when you confessed with your mouth the Lord Jesus and believed God raised Him from the dead.*

Even though believers receive righteousness when they are born again, many people for lack of teaching still think that they are unworthy to receive the goodness of God. This satanic belief keeps driving deeper and deeper into their subconscious minds. If my being worthy of God depended upon my own strength, I would be a great failure. I know that I am weak in myself and I know that I am unworthy in myself, but Christ has made me worthy. So, no matter how I feel or what my feeble mind tells me, I am strong and in Him I am worthy.

Ever since man was created, he has tried to work out his own righteousness and tried to do the kind of work which would make himself look good in the sight of God. The basic cry of the heart of man is to be righteous before God; so many Christians do all kinds of work to obtain righteousness, such as confessing their sins,

*Romans 10:9,10: "That if thou shalt confess with thy mouth the Lord Jesus, and shalt believe in thine heart that God hath raised him from the dead, thou shalt be saved. For with the heart man believeth unto righteousness; and with the mouth confession is made unto salvation."

teaching Sunday School classes and keeping the ten commandments. Yet these good works do not make a person righteous. Righteousness is obtained from God through the faith of Jesus Christ.

> Philippians 3:9:
> And be found in him, not having mine own righteousness, which is of the law, but that which is through the faith of Christ, the righteousness which is of God by faith [believing].

Your tears, your toil and all your prayers — your good works — will avail nothing. Righteousness is not by the cross that *you* bear, but by the cross that *Jesus Christ* bore for you. The righteousness of God is given to every believer, not of works, but by God's grace which is divine favor.

> II Corinthians 5:21:
> For he [God] hath made him [Jesus Christ] *to be* sin for us, who knew no sin; that we might be made the righteousness of God in him.

God made Jesus Christ to be sin for us. Jesus, who knew no sin, took our sin upon Himself so that we might be made the righteousness of God in Christ Jesus. Everything Adam lost in the fall,

Physical and Spiritual Wholeness

Jesus Christ regained for the believer when He died upon the cross.* Jesus Christ, who knew no sin, was made sin for us that we might be made the righteousness of God.

Today there is no longer a question of the sin problem. The sin problem was settled in Jesus Christ. What remains is the sinner's problem. A sinner, when he accepts Jesus Christ as Lord, must renew his mind to believe The Word that he is righteous, and as a son of God he will no longer worry, fear or feel unworthy. He will simply have confidence that he is worthy through Christ Jesus.

Many denominations have erroneously taught that a person can be righteous one minute and unrighteous the next; and if that person does not become righteous again before his death, he will miss heaven and end up in hell. This is not true. When God made us righteous in Christ Jesus over nineteen hundred years ago, we had nothing to do with it. When the Spirit of God in Christ is born within us, we are *at that moment* and *forevermore* righteous. We receive the nature of God which

---

*I Peter 2:24: "Who his own self bare our sins in his own body on the tree, that we, being dead to sins, should live unto righteousness: by whose stripes ye were healed."

makes us righteous right then and there.

Romans 3:22–25:

Even the righteousness of God *which is* by faith of Jesus Christ unto all and upon all them that believe: for there is no difference:

For all have sinned, and come short of the glory of God;

Being justified freely by his grace through the redemption that is in Christ Jesus:

Whom God hath set forth to be a propitiation [payment] through faith in his blood, to declare his righteousness for the remission of sins that are past, through the forbearance of God.

You cannot and I cannot earn this righteousness. God in Christ Jesus was made righteousness unto you over nineteen hundred years ago. So why do you still say, "I am an unrighteous person" if you are born again?

I Corinthians 1:30:

But of him [God] are ye in Christ Jesus, who of God is made unto us wisdom, and righteousness, and sanctification, and redemption.

You are not an unrighteous person if you are born of God for you have been made *righteous;* you have been given *wisdom;* you have been *sanctified* and you have been *redeemed.* I call this a gospel of deliverance. Neither you nor I by our own efforts can achieve this; it was "made unto us," done for us.

> Romans 5:8:
> But God commendeth [favorably introduced] his love toward us, in that, while we were yet sinners, Christ died for us.

Christ died for us, not when we were good enough, but when we were bad enough to need Him. And in making us righteous, Jesus Christ also spared us from future tribulation.

> Romans 5:9:
> Much more then, being now justified by his blood, we shall be saved from wrath through him [Christ].

How I love to teach this gospel of deliverance and righteousness. When you know you are righteous in Him, believe. When you believe the Word of God, you know that your life is in Him; then no fear, worry and guilt can frustrate and defeat you. For a believer there is no want, there is no poverty, there is no sickness, there is no defeat because these were overcome by way of Jesus Christ. You can be released from your bondage today if you but believe the Word of God. You must have confidence toward God.

> I John 3:20,21:
> For if our heart condemn us, God is greater than our heart, and knoweth all things.
>
> Beloved, if our heart condemn us not, *then* have we confidence toward God.

So long as man's heart, his innermost being, is condemning or accusing him for any reason, he cannot get answers to prayer because he does not have confidence toward God. He cannot believe and accept the simple promises of God's Word. Those who are righteous in Christ Jesus and who know that they are righteous have no reason to fear. They can have confidence toward God and therefore think and live victoriously.

CHAPTER NINE

The Broken Body and The Shed Blood
Healing in the Holy Communion

Great numbers of Christians are suffering from lack of strength and physical wholeness. Their lack of well-being is in most instances due to either wrong teaching or no teaching at all on the subject of this study. Most Christians are thoroughly familiar with the meaning of the shed blood but not with the broken body in the communion ceremony. The broken body aspect of the communion service deserves study and teaching.

The value of this study in abundant living depends entirely upon what position you hold regarding the Word of God. If you believe that the Bible is the Word of God and that it is God's answer to the needs of man, then you will be able to manifest the results in your life.

According to Malachi 3:6, God says, "For I *am* the Lord, I change not ...." He is the same all the time.

What He was once, He is always. What He did once, He does always. The God whom I know, whom I teach and preach, and for whom I labor is the same God as the God of Abraham, David and Paul. God has not become one bit weaker throughout these years.

The fruitfulness of this study, to a marked degree, depends upon whether or not you are seeking deliverance from sickness. If you are not seeking complete deliverance for your life but an excuse for bondage, this study will not be of profit to you. There are people who believe that it is God's will for them to be sick. There are people who believe that God is the author of sickness, suffering and all manner of evil to mankind. There are people who believe that God makes them better Christians by sending sickness and disease. All these positions are out-and-out contradictions of the Word of God. God does not send sickness, disease and sin into anyone's life in order to make him a more worthy or holy Christian, nor does God send sickness and disease to try people.

When the Corinthian church was manifesting sickness, division and strife, Paul did not applaud them for their sickness. He did not say, "It is a sign of God's love that you are sick." Nor did Paul say, "Bear your sickness patiently for God is trying you." The Apostle Paul, according to the Epistle to the Corinthians, rebuked them and endeavored to correct them for being sick. He rebuked them not as individuals but as a congregation, as Christians, because they did not properly *discern the Lord's body*. They did not realize that Jesus, who was sacrificed on the cross of Calvary, had accomplished something for them in His body. Paul pointed out that it was no longer necessary to suffer sickness and disease.

The age of Law was totally different from the age of the Church. Deuteronomy 28:15—61 tells about the curse of the law, those things which befell men who were disobedient to the law.

Deuteronomy 28:15:
But it shall come to pass, if thou wilt not hearken unto the voice of the Lord thy God, to observe to do all his commandments and his statutes which I command thee this day; that all these curses shall come upon thee, and overtake thee.

Verse 22:
The Lord shall smite thee with a consumption, and with a fever, and with an inflammation, and with an extreme burning ....

Verse 27:
The Lord will smite thee with the botch of

Egypt, and with the emerods, and with the scab, and with the itch, whereof thou canst not be healed.

Verse 28:
The Lord shall smite thee with madness, and blindness, and astonishment of heart.

Verse 35:
The Lord shall smite thee in the knees, and in the legs, with a sore botch that cannot be healed ....

Verse 60:
Moreover he will bring upon thee all the diseases of Egypt ....

Verse 61:
Also every sickness, and every plague ... them will the Lord bring upon thee ....

The great portion of this whole section is concerned with sickness and disease.

The Church, the body of believers, is no longer under the curse of the law. By the grace of God through Jesus Christ, we now are able to live the more abundant life.

Galatians 3:13:
Christ hath redeemed us from the curse of the
law, being made a curse for us: for it is written,
Cursed *is* every one that hangeth on a tree.

If we have been redeemed from the curse of the
law then we no longer have the curse upon us. "Christ
hath redeemed [past tense] us from the curse of the
law ...." That means He has redeemed us, not only
from *some* of the things mentioned in the curse, but
from *all* of them, which includes sickness and disease.

If the Church has been redeemed from sickness and
disease, why then was the Corinthian church sickly
and weak?

I Corinthians 11:29,30:
For he that eateth and drinketh unworthily,
eateth and drinketh damnation to himself, not
discerning the Lord's body.

For this cause many *are* weak and sickly among
you, and many sleep.

The Corinthian church was well aware of what the
blood of Christ meant, but they were failing to
discern the body of the Lord.

It is not stated how many members the Corinthian

Physical and Spiritual Wholeness

church had, but the number in another group from the Old Testament can be documented. Some scholars estimate that two and one half million people left Egypt, because there were 600,000 men plus their wives and children.*

> Psalm 105:37:
> ... *there was* not one feeble *person* among their tribes.

There is always something obviously wrong when members of the Church are weak and sickly and people are dying prematurely. If God can take two and a half million from Egypt without one feeble person among them, then what is there He cannot do in the day in which we live? Will God not do as much, if not more, in this age of Grace than He did in the time of the Law? This is a greater day to be alive than were the days of Moses.** Jesus Christ arose from the dead, the holy spirit is in the Christian people with great potential power.

The children of Israel had been in Egypt for four hundred years and had been terribly mistreated by

*Exodus 12:37: "And the children of Israel journeyed from Rameses to Succoth, about six hundred thousand on foot *that were* men, beside children."
** Acts 13:38,39: "Be it known unto you therefore, men *and* brethren, that through this man is preached unto you the forgiveness of sins: And by Him all that believe are justified from all things, from which ye could not be justified by the law of Moses."

the Egyptian slave masters.

> Exodus 2:23,24:
> And it came to pass in process of time, that the
> king of Egypt died: and the children of Israel
> sighed by reason of the bondage, and they cried,
> and their cry came up unto God by reason of
> the bondage.
>
> And God heard their groaning, and God remem-
> bered his covenant with Abraham, with Isaac,
> and with Jacob.

For 80 years Israel had been waiting for her de-
liverer to appear.

> Exodus 3:10:
> Come ... and I will send thee [Moses] unto
> Pharaoh, that thou mayest bring forth my
> people the children of Israel out of Egypt.

And God brought them out under the leadership of
a man called Moses. Moses became God's spokesman;
and in preparation for the freeing of the enslaved
Israelites, God instructed the people through His
spokesman.

> Exodus 12:3,6–8,11:
> Speak ye unto all the congregation of Israel,

81

saying ... take to them every man a lamb ....

... kill it in the evening.

And they shall take of the blood, and strike *it* on the two side posts and on the upper door post of the houses ....

And they shall eat the flesh in that night ....

... it *is* the Lord's passover.

God gave His Word; the results followed those who heard and believed.

God said to Moses that he should tell the people to do two things: (1) take the blood of the lamb and sprinkle it on the lintel and the side posts of the door and (2) eat the flesh. The blood and the flesh were equally important, equally significant, so far as the Word of God and the people of Israel were concerned. It was the Lord's Passover.

I want you to note something else. When the Lord passed over Egypt and the firstborn of the Egyptians were slain, God protected the homes of the children of Israel because of the blood they sprinkled on the lintel and side posts. Only the blood protected them. The account in Exodus does not mention anything about seeing a carcass or the flesh of the lamb laying outside the door. If any Hebrew father had said, "Oh, that Word of God which Moses is speaking is nonsense; I don't believe in that kind of stuff. It's foolish to kill a lamb and sprinkle the blood on our door lintel, and then think the destroyer will not come. I will not do it. I refuse to listen to Moses; he cannot be God's man." If the father had actually believed this, the eldest son of that family would have died along with the firstborn of the unbelieving Egyptians.

After affording protection to the children of Israel by the shedding of blood, what was the purpose of the command, "... Eat the flesh ..."? God told them to eat the flesh of the lamb so that their physical needs would be met. Looking at those Hebrews that night in Egypt, they did not appear changed on the outside. But something had happened because the Israelites acted upon God's Word.

Believing is indicated by acting upon what God has promised. The Hebrew people led by Moses demonstrated believing. God gave them physical wholeness when they ate the flesh of the lamb, and literally spared their lives because they followed His directions by sprinkling the blood. Not one second before they ate the lamb did they receive wholeness. But, that evening when they ate the flesh of the lamb, whose blood they had sprinkled on the lintel and the door posts, they ate physical health to themselves. The destroyer passed over without harming the obedient Israelites, and the next morning everyone was whole in every way.

These people acted upon the Word of God as it was spoken by Moses. Some of you are saying, "Well if there were a Moses today, I would believe." Would you? Whenever there is a man of God speaking the Word of God, you have the absolute Word. When I am preaching the gospel, I am God's man with His power in me, and everyone believing the words that I speak gets results when he acts upon them. This The Word promises.

Just as the blood of the lamb was the covering for the sins of the children of Israel, so the blood of Jesus Christ was shed for sin. The body of Christ was offered for the consequences of sin (that is, sickness, disease and want) just as the eating of the flesh was the healing for the physical needs of the children of Israel.

Matthew 8:17:
... Himself [Jesus] took our infirmities [unwholeness], and bare *our* sicknesses.

These two things Jesus did for us for *He is our Passover.*

84

The Broken Body and the Shed Blood

I Corinthians 5:7:

... For even Christ our passover is sacrified for us.

In the record of Exodus 12, Israel was beginning a journey from the land of Egypt, the land of slavery, to the promised land. In that journey one can find a true comparison to the journey of every person today. It depicts the journey a Christian may take from the time of slavery, defeat and frustration to the more abundant life. The only difference is that the children of Israel looked forward to the time of the cross of Jesus, while we look back to the accomplishments in the cross of Jesus.

How we have neglected to reach God's people with this truth about Jesus' bearing our sickness. We have taught that Jesus bore our sin but have neglected to teach the other half — that He "... bare *our* sicknesses." The Word of God is clear regarding these two definite parts in the death of Jesus. I am not preaching a new doctrine, I am not teaching a new gospel; I am teaching the gospel that Peter, Paul and the rest of the apostles taught and preached which brought deliverance to the believers. I believe in the complete work of Jesus Christ, not only for salvation from sin but salvation from sickness as well. If Peter can say, "... In the name of Jesus Christ ... rise up and walk," so can I, so can your pastor, so can you because The

Word says so. We are only limited to the extent that we limit the Word of God in us. He, Jesus Christ, bore our sickness and our sin.

The elements of the Passover for Israel are equivalent to Holy Communion for the Church. The Passover lamb had two important parts: blood and flesh. So also, the death of the lamb of God had two elements: blood and flesh, symbolized in Holy Communion by the cup and the bread.

> I Corinthians 10:16:
> The cup of blessing which we bless, is it not the communion of the blood of Christ? The bread which we break, is it not the communion of the body of Christ?

I Corinthians 10:16 has the two elements so clearly depicted; yet for years I missed the great physical healing power in Holy Communion. I always believed that "the celebration of the Lord's Supper has ever been regarded by the church as the innermost sanctuary of the whole Christian worship," as set forth in our Communion liturgy. But I had not been taught in the churches or seminaries I attended that the body of Jesus was given for my physical wholeness, although the Bible says it is so. Sickness has come upon the Church even though we partake of both elements because we have failed to properly discern the Lord's body.

> Psalms 103:3:
> Who [God] forgiveth all thine iniquities; who
> healeth all thy diseases.

There are two parts: sin and disease, one is removed by the blood of the lamb and the other by the
flesh of the lamb.

> Isaiah 53:5:
> But he *was* wounded for our transgressions, *he
> was* bruised for our iniquities: the chastisement
> of our peace *was* upon him; and with his stripes
> we are healed.

This passage prophesies the accomplishments of
the promised Messiah, Jesus Christ. Again, note the
two elements: forgiveness and healing. Wholeness has
two parts: spiritual and physical.

There are seven different names for God depicting
His nature in the Old Testament. One of the seven is
Jehovah Rapha which is Hebrew, meaning, "... I *am*
the Lord that healeth thee," as given in Exodus
15:26.

An integral part of the nature of God is physical
healing. The Lord, at the time the children of Israel

marched out of Egypt, gave them the promise, "I am the Lord that healeth thee." He is still the same Lord today. Satan causes sickness and disease. God made available salvation and healing.

> I Peter 2:24:
> Who his own self bare our sins in his own body on the tree, that we, being dead to sins, should live unto righteousness: by whose stripes ye were healed.

While Jesus had walked here upon earth demonstrating the will of God, the time came for the fulfillment of that which is recorded in II Corinthians.

> II Corinthians 5:21:
> For he hath made him *to be* sin for us, who knew no sin; that we might be made the righteousness of God in him.

Jesus who was without sin, was made sin for you and for me, "that we might be made the righteousness of God in him."

When describing the love shown at the crucifixion of Jesus, words fail. Jesus, the Son of God, without any sin – who did nothing but good for people, healing their broken bodies and giving them God's Word – now was to be crucified by them. They beat

Him and platted a crown of thorns to put on His head. They spit in His face and struck Him. Finally, they led Him up that rugged road to Calvary.

> John 19:17:
> And he bearing his cross went forth into a place called *the place* of a skull ....*

The cross Jesus bore was composed of everything that was against us.

> Colossians 2:14:
> Blotting out the handwriting of ordinances that was against us, which was contrary to us, and took it out of the way, nailing it to his cross.

It was that physical punishment which He went through that bought our healing. In Isaiah 53:5 we read, "with [by] his stripes we are healed," and in I Peter 2:24, "by whose stripes we were healed." Looking forward to the cross, Isaiah said that "we are healed." Peter looking back said, "by whose stripes we were healed [past tense]."

At the end of His earthly life when they were

---

*"And he [Jesus] bearing his cross" is the phrase from which has been inferred that Jesus bore the wooden cross. This does not agree with the clear record in the other three Gospels. They plainly stipulate that Simon of Cyrene bore the wooden cross from the door of the Judgment Hall.

beating Him and scourging Him, Jesus in His physical body was paying the price for the physical wholeness of mankind. When He allowed His body to be beaten and scourged, Jesus was redeeming us from sickness and disease. Not His body, but His blood was spilled at Calvary for the remission of sin.

> Matthew 26:28:
> For this is my blood of the new testament, which is shed for many for the remission of sins.

The term "shed blood" is a figure of speech and does not mean literally "to bleed," but that the life has gone from the blood. Jesus' blood was shed — He died — for the remission of sin, not for sickness.

Jesus was our complete substitute. He was our Passover. He was slain for us. Instead of having to live under the curse of the law, we now are free from that curse. We now live by grace through believing in the finished work of Jesus Christ, the Lamb of God.

When you and I believe and know our sonship rights in Christ, and when we know and believe in the total significance of Holy Communion, we will no longer tolerate sickness. Sickness and sin lose their power over us when we properly discern the Lord's body and blood.

90

The cup in Holy Communion represents the blood of Jesus Christ; the bread represents the body of Christ. Since Jesus bore my sin and sickness on Calvary's cross, then when I come to the Communion in remembrance of Him and eat of that bread and drink of that cup I have healing and forgiveness of sins because "his own self bare our sins in his own body on the tree ... by whose stripes ye were healed."

The Lord Jesus first instituted this new covenant of Holy Communion in symbolizing His blood and His body.

> I Corinthians 11:23–25:
> ... That the Lord Jesus the *same* night in which he was betrayed took bread:
>
> And when he had given thanks, he brake *it,* and said, Take, eat: this is my body, which is broken for you: this do in remembrance of me.
>
> After the same manner also *he took* the cup, when he had supped, saying, This cup is the new testament in my blood: this do ye, as oft as ye drink *it,* in remembrance of me.

The Corinthian church was admonished to continue celebrating the Lord's supper. After giving each element, the Scripture says, "this do in remembrance

91

of me." It is not just the "doing," but "doing in remembrance of Christ."

To have remembrance of anyone or anything, we must first have knowledge concerning that person or thing. We must know what Christ accomplished by his death before we can have a remembrance of the results of His suffering and death for us. Acting upon the promise of God brings the result that God said it would.

> Romans 10:11:
> The Scripture says, No man who believes in Him — who adheres to, relies on and trusts in Him — will [ever] be put to shame *or* be disappointed. (The Amplified New Testament.)

Go to the communion table knowing that your sins are forgiven and that by His stripes you were healed. It does not depend upon the feeling you may or may not have; it depends upon the accomplishments of Jesus Christ.

As the bread is served to you, remember that Christ said, "This is my body which is broken for you." By believing, receive and thank God for your physical as well as spiritual wholeness.

92

CHAPTER TEN

Complete In Him

Colossians 2:9,10:
For in him [Christ] dwelleth all the fulness of
the Godhead bodily.

And ye are complete in him ....

If we are complete in Christ then we are truly
complete. Few Christians have utilized the power of
God within them because they fail to renew their
minds to the absolute truth of The Word in believing
that they are complete. To live the more abundant
life and to be "more than conquerors through him
that loved us," we must confess and act as the Word
of God directs. When our confession fails to be in line
with The Word, we live below par, we fail to manifest
the more abundant life, and we do not indicate that
we are "more than conquerors." When we believe too
little, we manifest less than that which legally and
rightfully belongs to us as sons of God.

When I confess that I am not what His Word declares that I am, God is not less in me, but I am less in Him. Literally, it makes me a liar. I am then confessing that God is not right, and that He has not done for me what He says He has done. God forbid that we should do this for God is Truth and all men are liars.* If The Word declares that we are complete in Him then we are complete — for we are what The Word says we are, we have what it says we have, we will be what it says we will be, and we will have what it says we will have.

Our accepted English meaning of the word "complete" does not convey the proper emphasis in this phrase of the Scriptures: "And ye are complete in him ...." Aramaic better expresses this phrase with clarity.

In Aramaic there are four different grammatical forms to show the intensity of a verb. English has no verb form which corresponds to this Aramaic form. Even in Aramaic very few verbs go through all four of these conjugations.

---

*Romans 3:4: "God forbid: yea, let God be true, but every man a liar; as it is written, That thou mightest be justified in thy sayings, and mightest overcome when thou art judged."
I John 5:10: "He that believeth on the Son of God hath the witness in himself: he that believeth not God hath made him a liar; because he believeth not the record that God gave of his Son."

The first conjugation is *Peal* in Hebrew, *Peshitta* in Estrangelo Aramaic, or what would be a simple form in English. The second conjugation is called *Pael* in Hebrew, *Marcobta* in Estrangelo Aramaic, or what would be an intensive form in English. The third conjugation is called *Aphel* in the Hebrew, *Yatair Marcobta* in Estrangelo Aramaic, or what would be an extensive form in English. To show some sort of comparison with English, we will use the passive verb "to be complete." The intensive form would show a more intense completion — "to be completely complete." The extensive form indicates even more intensity — "completely and absolutely complete."

If in Colossians 2:10 God had put the verb "complete" in this last (extensive) usage — namely, that we are "completely and absolutely complete in Him" — it would be very wonderful; but this is not the case. God goes beyond even this extensive form to show us how complete we are in Him. The Aramaic manuscripts use in Colossians 2:10 a very rare fourth conjugation.

This fourth conjugation is called *Shaphel* in the Hebrew, *Yatair Yatair Marcobta* in Estrangelo Aramaic, or what would be an extra extensive form in English. It is found only a few times in the Bible. This conjugation, very rarely used, is difficult to translate. But here is an attempt to translate Colossians 2:10 as it is given in the *Eshtaphal* (passive form of *Shaphel*) form from the Aramaic: "We are completely, completely, absolutely complete in Him!" Such completeness is incomprehensible to the finite human mind. At best, we can know for a certainty that we are lacking in nothing.

The following are some of the ways which make up our completeness.

Colossians 1:12,13:
Giving thanks unto the Father, which hath made us meet to be partakers of the inheritance of the saints in light:

Who hath delivered us from the power of darkness, and hath translated *us* into the kingdom of [by] his dear Son.*

Colossians 1:21,22:
And you, that were sometime alienated and enemies in *your* mind by wicked works, yet now hath he reconciled.

In the body of his flesh through death, to present you holy and unblameable and unreproveable in his sight.

Ephesians 1:7:
In whom we have redemption through his blood,

*Colossians 1:13: "Who hath rescued us out from among the exercise or operative influence of darkness (kingdom) and separated us, bringing us as citizens into His kingdom by the work of His dear son. (literal translation according to usage)

the forgiveness of sins, according to the riches of his grace.

I Corinthians 1:30:
But of him [God] are ye in Christ Jesus, who of God is made unto us wisdom, and righteousness, and sanctification, and redemption.

Colossians 2:10–12:
And ye are complete in him, which is the head of all principality and power:

In whom also ye are circumcised with the circumcision made without hands, in putting off the body of the sins of the flesh by the circumcision of Christ:

Buried with him in baptism, wherein also ye are risen with *him* through the faith of the operation of God, who hath raised him from the dead.

Romans 8:37:
Nay, in all these things we are more than conquerors through him that loved us.

Romans 6:4:
Therefore, we are buried with him by baptism into death: that like as Christ was raised up from the dead by the glory of the Father, even so we also should walk in newness of life.

Physical and Spiritual Wholeness

As born-again sons of God, we are *complete* in Him. The next step is to manifest this completeness. The operation of the gift of holy spirit in each born-again believer is the key to unleashing potential power and demonstrating completeness. The gift of the holy spirit has nine manifestations which are set forth in I Corinthians 12.

> I Corinthians 12:7–11:
> But the manifestation of the Spirit is given to every man to profit withal.
>
> For to one is given by the Spirit the word of wisdom; to another the word of knowledge by the same Spirit;
>
> To another faith by the same Spirit; to another the gifts of healing by the same Spirit;
>
> To another the working of miracles; to another prophecy; to another discerning of spirits; to another *divers* kinds of tongues; to another the interpretation of tongues:
>
> But all these worketh that one and the selfsame Spirit, dividing to every man severally [his own] as he [the man] will.

When we operate these manifestations, we begin to evidence some of our God-given power. To go a step further, the manifestations of the spirit result in producing fruit of the spirit.

> Galatians 5:22,23:
> But the fruit of the Spirit is love, joy, peace, longsuffering, gentleness, goodness, faith,
>
> Meekness, temperance ....

Fruit results from the operation of the manifestations of the spirit. Christians can no more show the fruit of the spirit without operating the manifestations of the spirit than they can manifest the spirit without having the spirit. Fruit of the spirit, of which Galatians 5:22 and 23 speak, is not the fruit of man's works. The fruit which evidences itself upon the operation of the manifestations of the spirit is the only "fruit of the spirit." First we operate the manifestations, the tools, and thereby cultivate into evidence the fruit. This truth is remarkable when we consider that for years we have read "fruit of the spirit" but have consistently acted as if it should have read "the fruit of the works of man."

How truly wonderful it is to realize that as sons of God we have the manifestations of the spirit and that by the operation of these manifestations is evidenced the fruit of the spirit. The fruit of the spirit comes into manifestation in the senses world only as we renew our minds to act by the power of the spirit within us. Often people who appear to be producing fruit by their works, even though it looks like genuine fruit, are producing the works of man and not the fruit of the spirit. We as Christians are warned of being deceived by such.

Colossians 2:8:
Beware lest any man spoil you through philosophy and vain deceit, after the tradition of men, after the rudiments of the world, and not after Christ.

Colossians 2:4:
And this I say, lest any man should beguile you with enticing words.

The manifestations of the spirit and the evidencing of the fruit of the spirit show forth some of our completeness. The full extent of being "complete in him," however, can only be known when we see Him face to face.

Colossians 3:1—4:
If ye then be risen with Christ, seek those things which are above, where Christ sitteth on the right hand of God.

Set your affection on things above, not on things on the earth.

For ye are dead, and your life is hid with Christ in God.

When Christ, *who is* our life, shall appear, then shall ye also appear with him in glory.

Surely when we "appear with him in glory," we shall be able to fully appreciate that we are completely, completely, absolutely complete in Him. How spiritually invigorating it is to know and to realize that we as Christians are what God says we are and that we have what He says we have. We must renew our minds to believe and appropriate His Word to our every day living.

Part IV

The Word
in Our Minds

Part IV

The Word in Our Minds

The purpose of the third part, "Physical and Spiritual Wholeness," of *The Bible Tells Me So* was to make us strong by showing how well God has taken care of our every need. Part I, as our point of departure, began by caring for our mental health. We need mental freedom and wholeness before we can launch into understanding God's other truths. Next, in Part II, we saw the simplicity and power of the law of believing which works, knowingly or unknowingly, for absolutely everyone. All the truths in the first three parts are clearly documented and explained in God's Word. However, on the subjects in this Part IV, the clarity of God's Word has been muddied by passage of time, translations and interpretations. So now we must again study the Word of God and look for clarity on subjects which have been relatively unstudied or on subjects which have been grossly misunderstood and thus inaccurately taught.

The following eight studies on the accuracy of the

Word of God begin with the less complicated but dynamic subjects — "The Palms of God," "Walk of Youth" — and progressively delve into the deeper research of "The Bondage of the Sabbath," "Baptism," "Paul's Thorn in the Flesh," "When Judas Hanged Himself" and "Study — Be Diligent."

The capstone of delight and study is the final chapter of "As He Is" — a study of the three words *as He is* from I John. These words show us the incredible truth that "as he is so are we in this world." Since we are as He is, our mental freedom, our positive believing, our completeness both physically and spiritually should rally with excitement and strength. This is what happens when we put His Word in our minds.

CHAPTER ELEVEN

The Palms of God

The figure of speech *condescensio** in "the palms of God," is most beautifully used in Isaiah, as an Orientalism in all of its significance.

> Isaiah 49:15,16:
> Can a woman forget her sucking child, that she should not have compassion on the son of her womb? yea, they may forget, yet will I not forget thee.
>
> Behold, I have graven [tattooed] thee upon the palms of *my* hands; thy walls [hands] *are* continually before me.

Motherhood is an unforgettable human experience. A mother nursing her new-born child has indescribable feelings of attachment and tender affection for the fruit of her womb. Yet, God says that a woman could forget her baby — which is most difficult and

---

*Condescensio — This figure of speech attributes human characteristics to God — "palms of God."

unlikely — but God will never forget one of His own. To emphasize God's great ability to remember His children, this passage states that God's remembrance is beyond that of a mother for her child. God's memory is even deeper than the memory of a most intimate human relationship. God's memory of us is beyond human comprehension.

After this dramatic statement of God's remembering His children, verse 16 of Isaiah 49 uses a graphic figure of speech attributing to God the human characteristic of palms: "I have graven thee upon the palms of *my* hands." The Oriental way of expressing great love and continual remembrance is by engraving which we would call tattooing. The Oriental tradition was to tattoo on your body the names of those you dearly love while simply giving presents to those you love slightly.

The process of tattooing is very unpleasant. Whenever a person is tattooed, it is usually on the arm, sometimes on the back or chest. But never do you see the palms of a man's hand tattooed. Why? Because the palms of the hands are too sensitive. They are too delicate. The pain of tattooing on the palms is too great to bear. Yet God says, "Behold, I have graven thee upon the palms of *my* hands." First of all, God is saying it takes too long to look on the arm or on the shoulders or across the chest, because that part of the body is clothed with various types of garments;

therefore, He has tattooed us upon the palms of His hands. There He can see us constantly. God loves us so much that, figuratively, He is willing to bear the excruciating pain of having us tattooed on the palms of His hands. It isn't too painful for God to engrave our names upon the palms of His hands because we are dearly beloved of Him.

> John 3:16:
> For God so loved the world, that he gave his only begotten Son, that whosoever believeth in him should not perish, but have everlasting life.

God is trying to illustrate how much He cares for us by saying, "Behold, I have graven thee upon the palms of *my* hands." He is saying that He has taken a most delicate, a most sensitive part of His being, and there He has tattooed our names. In reality He is saying, "I love you so much I don't want my love to be hidden underneath the garments, I don't want my love to be covered so that it cannot be seen; but I have graven you on a most delicate and sensitive part of my being that at any time I look I can see you." That is the love of God. When you see the beauty of this Scripture you will begin to appreciate the compassion and love of God.

The second part of this truth says, "... thy walls *are* continually before me." The word "walls" is a very inaccurate presentation. The palms of the hands are the walls. When you lift them up they are walls before your face.

Besides having us engraved on His palms, our own palms are continually before Him. What does God see in the palms of our hands? He sees on them nothing but sin, doubt, fear, bitterness, quarrels, lies, hatred – everything that stains a sinner. He sees on our palms the fear of death, the fear of disease and sickness, the insecurity and uncertainty of the future. Yet God in His wonderful infinite love, irrespective of who we were, tattooed or engraved us on His palms.

God's continuous remembrance of His children is true because He has engraved them, His children, upon the palms of His hands.

> Isaiah 1:18:
> Come now, and let us reason together, saith the Lord: though your sins be as scarlet, they shall be as white as snow; though they be red like crimson, they shall be as wool.

This is part of the significance of God's continuous remembrance.

> Isaiah 43:25:
> I, *even* I, *am* he that blotteth out thy trans-

gressions for mine own sake, and will not remember thy sins.

Psalms 103:12:
As far as the east is from the west, *so* far hath he removed our transgressions from us.

Wouldn't you say that God certainly has engraved us upon the palms of His hands? He forgives and forgets our shortcomings while He remembers and cares for us constantly.

God gives us in Revelation a comparable truth.

Revelation 3:20:
Behold, I stand at the door, and knock: if any man hear my voice, and open the door, I will come in to him, and will sup [eat] with him, and he with me.

Have you ever thought on the beauty of those words? In the Orient the host does not eat with his guest unless he is a most intimate friend. In this passage of Scripture Jesus is saying, "I am your most intimate friend." Jesus enters into our hearts upon our invitation. He never forces Himself on us. He is not just entering in, but He is supping with us. Jesus said, "I want to be very intimate with my people; I will sup with them; I will eat with them if they will but ask Me."

Hebrews 13:5 says, "... I will never leave thee, nor forsake thee." Also Matthew 28:20 says, "... lo, I am with you alway, *even* unto the end of the world."

The Lord is with us always. That is why He said as recorded in Matthew 11:28, "Come unto me, all *ye* that labour and are heavy laden, and I will give you rest." It is God's continuous remembrance whereby He can say to us, "I have graven you upon the palms of my hands even though your walls, your palms, are continually before me."

Christ died for all and thus He could say, "Whosoever will may come." Once Christ has offered the invitation, it is a matter of our accepting it. If you want to come to Christ you may. Man need not die in his sin because Christ died for sin and carried our sicknesses and our pains. We need not carry them. God has willingly and gladly engraved our names upon the palms of His hands.

There is no question about the call of Jesus Christ to man being clear. The only question is whether man is going to respond to that call. When Jesus died upon Calvary's cross, He died for everybody in the whole world; but only those who accept Him as their Savior receive the benefits of His death.

Those of us who have accepted Jesus as Lord in

our lives — we have been engraved in the palms of God's hands. He continuously remembers and watches over us. Do you remember "... that whosoever believeth in Him should not perish, but have everlasting life"? He has come to abide within us forever, that we may have eternal life now and forevermore.

This is God's continuous remembrance of us. There is not a day, hour, minute or second when we as sons of God are not remembered before the throne of God. We sons of God have truly been engraved on the *palms of God*.

CHAPTER TWELVE

The Walk of Youth

In this day and age, the actions of youth are being closely watched. It is fitting, therefore, that we take a good look at a verse of Scripture in the first epistle to Timothy which clearly sets forth the importance and responsibility of the younger generation.

> I Timothy 4:12:
> Let no man despise thy youth; but be thou an example of the believers, in word, in conversation, in charity, in spirit, in faith, in purity.

Let us take this verse line by line and word by word in order to see the true beauty in the accuracy of God's matchless Word.

"Let no man despise thy youth." The word "man" is an inclusive noun. We are told to allow no one, Christian or non-Christian, believer or unbeliever, to despise our youth. The word "despise" means "to think disparagingly of."

Matthew 18:10:
Take heed that ye despise not [think disparagingly of] one of these little ones.

Young people are to so condition their thinking, their work and their pattern of living, that no one can think disparagingly of them.

In the Biblical usage of the word "youth" lies an illuminating truth. In the Bible a young person is referred to as a youth until he reaches thirty years of age. According to Jewish custom no person was allowed to teach until he was thirty years old nor was he considered for membership in the Sanhedrin (ruling body of Israel) until he had reached thirty. Abraham took Isaac to the top of Mount Moriah when Isaac was thirty years of age. Joseph was thirty when Pharaoh appointed him ruler of Egypt. Jesus did not begin His teaching ministry until reaching the age of thirty. This same word "youth" is used in the Gospels when Jesus was talking to the rich young ruler (Matthew 19:20; Mark 10:20; Luke 18:21). This man was very wealthy and yet only a youth under thirty years old.

The word "but" in I Timothy 4:12 sets that which precedes in contrast with that which follows, "but be thou [youth] an example." The word "be" means "to become or to come into a particular state or condition." This, then, expresses a growing process —

114

a state of not having fully arrived, but of becoming or in the process of arriving.

The word "example" comes from the Greek word *tupos* which, transliterated into English, becomes "type." "Of the believers" is the genitive of possession, literally translated "be thou a believer's example." Christian young people are to become believers' examples or types in six ways: (1) in word, (2) in conversation, (3) in charity, (4) in spirit, (5) in faith, (6) in purity. The preposition "in" is the same for each word and expresses an innermost depth, an inner quietness or self-reliance. Youths are to become, within the innermost part of their being, an example of quietness and serenity due to The Word's dwelling in them. This is not surprising, for it is God's Word which gives youths the knowledge they need regarding every phase of their life; it is The Word which God set above His Name.*

Youths are to become an example of the believers in conversation. The word "conversation" is the Greek word *anastrophē*, which means behavior or conduct. This behavior or conduct is like a straight line, conditioned and built upon the knowledge of The Word which is living within.

---

*Psalm 138:2: "... for thou hast magnified thy word above all thy name."

115

Galatians 1:13:
For ye have heard of my conversation
[behavior – *anastrophē*] in time past.

Youths are to become an example of the believers
in charity. The word "charity" is the Greek word
agapē, which means the love of God in the renewed
mind in manifestation. The walk of youth is first of
all with the inner quietness or serenity of The Word,
secondly in a behavior that is straight without wavering or fluctuating and thirdly with the love of God in
the renewed mind in manifestation.

The words "in spirit" which appear in the King
James Version do not appear in the critical Greek
texts of Griesbach, Lachmann, Tischendorf, Tregelles,
Alford, Wordsworth or Nestle; nor do they appear in
any of the Aramaic texts. Therefore, "in spirit"
should be deleted.

The word "faith" is the Greek word *pistis* and is
translated either "faith" or "believing." Faith is
spiritual, within an individual; believing connotes
action. If the youths are to become examples, it must
be by their actions. Therefore, *pistis* in this verse
should be translated believing. Young people are to
become examples in their believing action.

The word "purity" is the Greek word *hagneia*,

which means "chastity." But chastity, normally construed as meaning pure, really does not fit if taken in the context of the verse. The root of this word is *hagnos*, meaning "to keep lustrous" even though living in this present tarnished world. This word is used referring to Jesus Christ in I John 3:3, "even as he [Jesus Christ] is pure [*hagnos*]." Jesus Christ was in the flesh in this world, but the world was not mixed in Him to the end that He was contaminated.

Another closely aligned Greek word is *hēgeomai*. This word is also used of a Roman provincial governor, a principal leader who is uncontaminated by what others say. Youths are to walk as leaders, in a straight line, uncontaminated by others. It is a pure walk.

How beautiful and how accurate is God's matchless Word. After studying and understanding the depth of I Timothy 4:12, the following literal translation according to usage is offered.

Allow no one to think disparagingly of you as a youth. Become a believer's example in the quietness, serenity and self-composure you have within yourself because of your study and knowledge of the rightly divided, revealed Word. Become an example in your behavior and manner of life. Become an example in the love

117

of God in the renewed mind in manifestation. Become an example in believing action in your life. Become an example in your uncontaminated leadership.

Young people have been given a great challenge *by* God's Word and great responsibility *to* His Word. In the youth lie wells of abilities and qualities. God commands them to perfect and use their potential to benefit themselves and the entire Church.

CHAPTER THIRTEEN

The Bondage of the Sabbath Day

It is folly for a Christian to try to live under a law or laws which no longer exist. This situation is like stopping at a corner after the stop sign has been removed. You can stop, but you don't have to. This is similar to Christians who adhere to keeping the Sabbath. Tradition must not blind us and keep us unaware of changes which occur as the Word of God progresses from one age to the next.

The laws of the Sabbath were given *to* Israel and, therefore, apply *to* Israel. Since these laws were never given *to* the Church, their interpretation cannot be *for* it. The Sabbath laws were applied *to* and *for* Israel and as such were never altered, changed or transferred to any other period.

The Scriptures clearly state that we as born-again sons of God are not under law, but grace.

The Word in Our Minds

Romans 7:4:
Wherefore, my brethren, ye also are become dead to the law by [on account of] the body of Christ....

How could the law possibly have power over us when the law is dead?

People trying to live under a law which does not pertain to them is not new in the Christian age. Paul had such in the church at Galatia.

Galatians 4:31:
So then, brethren, we are not children of the bondwoman, but of the free.

Galatians 5:1:
Stand fast therefore in the liberty wherewith Christ hath made us free, and be not entangled again with the yoke of bondage.

Galatians 4:9–11:
But now, after that ye have known God, or rather are known of God, how turn ye again to the weak and beggarly elements [including the law], whereunto ye desire again to be in bondage?

Ye observe days, and months, and times, and years.

I am afraid of you, lest I have bestowed upon you labour in vain.

Romans 14:5,6:
One man esteemeth one day above another: another esteemeth every day *alike*. Let every man be fully persuaded in his own mind.

He that regardeth the day, regardeth *it* unto the Lord; and he that regardeth not the day, to the Lord he doth not regard *it*. He that eateth, eateth to the Lord, for he giveth God thanks; and he that eateth not, to the Lord he eateth not, and giveth God thanks.

Colossians 2:16:
Let no man therefore judge you in meat, or in drink, or in respect of an holyday, or of the new moon, or of the sabbath *days*.

The vast majority of born-again believers assemble to worship on Sunday, on which day Jesus was first seen in His resurrected body. Simply because most of us observe Sunday does not mean we keep it under the compulsion of the law; we keep it because we are under grace and wish to do so. In our age, during the

Church Administration, every day is sacred according to the Word of God and not one day more so than any other day. Each day should be lived unto the Lord, though in our tradition most Christians have set aside Sunday especially as a day of rest and special worship.

* * * * *

Besides the Sabbath, other days spoken of in the Bible also need clarification, specifically "man's day," "Christ's day," and the "Lord's day."

Man's day pertains to now, the age of Grace. Man today passes judgment and sentence; he directs the policy.

> I Corinthians 4:3:
> But with me it is a very small thing that I should be judged of you, or of man's judgment: yea, I judge not mine own self.

In the King James Version the word "day" is translated "judgment." In essence this word "judgment" expresses the truth that in man's day man does sit in judgment but only for a brief period.

Christ's Day is coming. In that day Christ will come for His Church; He will gather the dead in Christ and those believers who are yet alive.

122

Philippians 1:6,10:
Being confident of this very thing, that he which
hath begun a good work in you will perform *it*
until the day of Jesus Christ.

That ye may approve things that are excellent;
that ye may be sincere and without offence till
the day of Christ.

Philippians 2:16:
Holding forth the word of life; that I may rejoice
in the day of Christ, that I have not run in vain,
neither laboured in vain.

The Lord's Day (or the Day of the Lord) is not a
day of the week as has been commonly believed. It is
not Sunday. But, the Lord's Day is His Day on earth,
when the Lord Himself shall rule in righteousness and
power and glory. The Apostle John was shown this
Day in the distant future.

Revelation 1:10:
I was in the Spirit on the Lord's day, and heard
behind me a great voice, as of a trumpet.

As I Thessalonians informs us, that Day will not
overtake us born-again believers as a thief, for we are
not in darkness but we are the children of light.

I Thessalonians 5:2—5:

For yourselves know perfectly that the day of the Lord so cometh as a thief in the night.

For when they shall say, Peace and safety; then sudden destruction cometh upon them, as travail upon a woman with child, and they shall not escape.

But ye, brethren, are not in darkness, that that day should overtake you as a thief.

Ye are all the children of light, and the children of the day: we are not of the night, nor of darkness.

When we rightly divide the Word of Truth, we clear the atmosphere of the wrong teaching regarding the Sabbath and the other days mentioned in the Bible. We are not believers tied to one legalistic day of worship. We worship God daily in spirit and in truth. Tradition dare not blind us to the truth of the light of God's Word.

CHAPTER FOURTEEN

Baptism

Many of today's religious groups were founded upon various beliefs regarding baptism. This study allows the Scripture to speak for itself regarding the subject of baptism and will allow the reader to see for himself the great accuracy of the Word of God without the interpretational and doctrinal inconsistencies brought to the subject by man. Let us begin by examining the word "baptism," and then continue by tracing the use of water in baptism from the Old Testament, as it related to the law, to the present.

To discover the true meaning of "baptism," we must search the Scriptures and observe its varied usages. Of course, "baptism" *now* is an English word; the Greek *baptisma* is directly transliterated into English. The root form of the word *baptisma* is *baptō,* which means "to dip." *Baptō* is also part of the word translated "dippeth," *embaptō.*

The Word in Our Minds

From this root *baptō* arise four words:

1. *Baptizō* — to make things *baptō*, dipped.

2. *Baptismos* — the act of dipping or washing which is the act of baptizing; this does not occur in any Church epistle; the four occurrences of this word are in Mark 7:4; 7:8; Hebrews 6:2; 9:10.

3. *Baptisma* — the result of *baptismos;* it is used twenty-two times in the Bible: thirteen refer to John's baptism, five to the Lord's baptism, three are found in Paul's epistles, and the last is in Peter. *Baptisma* is in Matthew 3:7; 20:22,23; 21:25; Mark 1:4; 10:38,39; 11:30; Luke 3:3; 7:29; 12:50; 20:4; Acts 1:22; 10:37; 13:24; 18:25; 19:3,4; Romans 6:4; Ephesians 4:5; Colossians 2:12; I Peter 3:21.

4. *Baptistēs* — the one who does the baptizing.

There are only a few instances where these words are not directly transliterated into English as "baptize," but are instead translated as follows:

1. *Baptō* is translated "dip" in the only three places where it is used.

Luke 16:24:

And he cried and said, Father Abraham, have mercy on me, and send Lazarus, that he may dip [*baptō*] the tip of his finger in water, and cool my tongue; for I am tormented in this flame.

John 13:26:

Jesus answered, He it is, to whom I shall give a sop, when I have dipped [*baptō*] *it* ....

Revelation 19:13:

And he *was* clothed with a vesture dipped [*baptō*] in blood: and his name is called The Word of God.

2. *Embaptō* is translated as follows in its only usages.

Matthew 26:23:

And he answered and said, He that dippeth [*embaptō*] *his* hand with me in the dish, the same shall betray me.

Mark 14:20:

And he answered and said unto them, *It is* one of the twelve, that dippeth [*embaptō*] with me in the dish.

127

John 13:26:
Jesus answered, He it is, to whom I shall give a sop, when I have dipped [*baptō*] *it.* And when he had dipped [*embaptō*] the sop, he gave *it* to Judas Iscariot, *the son* of Simon [*Baptō* is used in both instances in John 13:26 in several critical Greek texts.]

3. *Baptizō* is consistently transliterated "baptize" except in three usages.

Mark 6:14:
And king Herod heard *of him;* (for his name was spread abroad:) and he said, That John the Baptist [*baptizō*]* was risen from the dead, and therefore mighty works do shew forth themselves in him.

Mark 7:4:
And *when they come* from the market, except they wash [*baptizō*], they eat not ....

Luke 11:38:
And when the Pharisee saw *it,* he marvelled that he had not first washed [*baptizō*] before dinner.

*The form of this word *baptizō* is the participle with the article. It is accurately translated "the one who baptizes."

In these last two usages the action is self-evident; when a Pharisee returned from the market, he washed himself before eating.

4. Of the four uses of *baptismos* it is only once translated "baptism" — Hebrews 6:2. In the other occurrences both the Authorized and Revised Versions are correct in rendering the word *baptismos* as "washing." The references are quite clear because they refer to the ordinances of divine service which were carried on in the tabernacle.

Mark 7:4:
And *when they come* from the market, except they wash, they eat not. And many other things there be, which they have received to hold, *as* the washing [*baptismos*] of cups, and pots, brasen vessels, and of tables.

Mark 7:8:
For laying aside the commandment of God, ye hold the tradition of men, *as* the washing [*baptismos*] of pots and cups: and many other such like things ye do.

Hebrews 9:10:
Which stood [serving] only in meats and

129

> drinks, and divers washings [*baptismos*], and carnal ordinances, imposed *on them* until the time of reformation [rectification]."

From every Biblical usage of the word "baptism," we can only conclude that the root meaning and the basic thought in baptism is washing. Therefore, we should note three other words in the Greek which also mean "to wash."

1. *Niptō* — to wash a portion of one's body.

> Matthew 15:2:
> Why do thy disciples transgress the tradition of the elders? for they wash not their hands when they eat bread.

2. *Louō* — to bathe or wash the entire body; from which we also get our word "ablution."

> Hebrews 10:22:
> Let us draw near with a true heart in full assurance of faith, having our hearts sprinkled from an evil conscience, and our bodies washed with pure water.

3. *Plunō* — to wash or rinse inanimate things; ordinarily this word is used in speaking of

washing clothes.

> Revelation 7:14:
> And I said unto him, Sir, thou knowest.
> And he said to me, These are they which
> came out of great tribulation, and have
> washed their robes, and made them white
> in the blood of the Lamb.

These three Greek words fully cover the subject of
washing. The word "wash" is used in the definition of
each one of the above words. Therefore, we must
logically conclude that the verb *baptizō* has a
meaning in common with all of these three afore-
mentioned Greek words, yet must be distinct from
each. A close study of each usage of *baptizō* reveals
that *baptizō* does not denote the removal of bodily
uncleanness or filth, but rather the removal of
ceremonial uncleanness and is symbolic washing. The
outward cleansing of the flesh by washing or baptism
was to symbolize spiritual cleanliness. Entrance into
the tabernacle was conditioned by baptism which
meant the cleansing of the flesh at the laver by
merely dipping to indicate ceremonial washing or
cleansing. (See Exodus 30:18–24.)

Exactly what means were used outside the temple
for washing? The Old Testament tells of the laver of
the tabernacle (Exodus 30:17–21), the sea and the

ten lavers of Solomon's temple (I Kings 7:23–39)
and the river of the temple (Ezekiel 47:1–12).

In the court of the tabernacle between the gate and
the door stood two vessels – the altar and the laver
(Exodus 40:29,30). Considering the minute detail
and exactness of the patterns shown to Moses regarding the tabernacle (Exodus 30:1–10), it is
interesting to note that the laver of the tabernacle
was not given dimensions or proportions but The
Word simply states what it was for – "to wash *withal*"
(Exodus 30:18). The fact that the details are missing
regarding the laver emphasizes the fact that it was not
an integral part of the completed structure and that
something better would come to replace it.

The temple of Solomon replaced the tabernacle.
This temple of Solomon had no single laver between
the entrance of the gate to the outer area and the
door of the temple, but had instead the sea and the
ten lavers, five on each side of the house (I Kings
7:23,38,39). The ten lavers were used to wash the
offering and they were set on bases each having "four
brasen wheels" (I Kings 7:30). Again the wheels
indicate easy disposal; they could roll out of the way
for something more permanent.

In the temple of Ezekiel, which is yet to come to
pass in the future, the lavers and the sea will be

132

removed and in their place, issuing from under the threshold of the house, will flow the river of living water (Ezekiel 47:1—5). Ezekiel's temple will not have water in containers, but a moving, living river, deepening as it flows (Ezekiel 47:3—5). Thus, in the course of God's plan we see that the lavers are all alike until finally lost in the river of living water.

The ceremonial cleansing, called washing and baptism, applies specifically to Israel. The laver of the tabernacle, the sea and the ten lavers of Solomon's temple, and the river of Ezekiel are all applicable to Israel — the first two under the Old Testament and the latter in the future when paradise is reestablished on earth. These two times which apply only to Israel are together Biblically called the kingdom period. The question thus becomes: What about baptism in the period of time between the law and the new paradise, between the time of Solomon's temple and the river of Ezekiel?

The day of Pentecost founded a new period or administration. At that time another change came in relation to baptism regarding the Church. In order to see exactly what this change meant, let us begin ten days before Pentecost at the time of the ascension in Acts 1.

The Word in Our Minds

>Acts 1:4,5:
>And, being assembled together with *them* [the apostles], [Jesus Christ] commanded them that they should not depart from Jerusalem, but wait for the promise of the Father, which, *saith he,* ye have heard of me.
>
>For John truly baptized with water; but ye shall be baptized with the Holy Ghost not many days hence.

In other words, with the coming of the greater (holy spirit), the lesser (water) came to an end. This replacement was initiated on Pentecost. On Pentecost the replacement first applied.

>Galatians 3:27,28:
>For as many of you as have been baptized into Christ have put on Christ.
>There is neither Jew nor Greek, there is neither bond nor free, there is neither male nor female: for ye are all one in Christ Jesus.*

Being baptized into the body of Christ doesn't mean baptized with the old physical element of water, but with the new spiritual element of holy spirit.

*The word "Jew" and its derivatives, as used in the King James Version, should always be understood as meaning "Judean" or "of the Judean religion." The word "Jew" was never used in any text until 1775.

134

I John 1:7:

But if we walk in the light, as he is in the light, we have fellowship one with another, and the blood of Jesus Christ his Son cleanseth us from all sin.*

Christ has done the cleansing for us. Our only work is to accept Him. He then washes away our sin.

The records of baptism in Acts, the book which records the events of Pentecost and immediately thereafter, do not mention water at all; thus to say there is water involved in baptism can only be private interpretation. In Acts 2:38 Peter baptized "in the name of Jesus Christ." In Acts 8:16 people were "baptized in the name of the Lord Jesus." In Acts 9:18, "he [Paul] received sight forthwith, and arose, and was baptized." And in Acts 19:5, "When they heard *this,* they were baptized in the name of the Lord Jesus."

If we are to rightly divide the Word of God, we must allow the Bible to speak for itself and not read into it the theologies and doctrines of men. Nowadays whenever the word "baptize" is mentioned, water is immediately associated with it because of the

---

*Then there is no more consciousness of sin as told in Hebrews 10:2: "For then would they not have ceased to be offered? because that the worshippers once purged should have had no more conscience of sins."

influence of religious doctrines, but we have just seen by examination of the above verses of Scripture that water is never stated.

On the other hand, even though we have these accounts which so clearly show that water was no longer necessary after the day of Pentecost, there are other Scriptural accounts which imply the use of water in baptism and which must be considered.

Peter speaks of water in Acts 10.

> Acts 10:47:
> Can any man forbid water, that these should not be baptized, which have received the Holy Ghost as well as we?

This is the same Peter who spoke in Acts 2:38. Why did he include water in Acts 10 when earlier he did not? In Acts 2:38 he did not have time to go to his office and prepare a sermon; he spoke by revelation and inspiration. But after the day of Pentecost, Peter was preaching in the synagogue and was still influenced by it. He simply reverted to his previous doctrine and added water. Peter himself clarifies this same account later in Acts 11.

> Acts 11:16:
> Then remembered I [after I had ordered water

baptism] the word of the Lord, how that he said, John indeed baptized with water; but ye shall be baptized with the Holy Ghost.

This record indicates he did not baptize the Cornelius household of believers in water.

In Acts 19 Paul asked certain disciples at Ephesus regarding what Apollos did.

Acts 19:2,3:
... Have ye received the Holy Ghost since [when] ye believed? And they said unto him, We have not so much as heard whether there be any Holy Ghost.

And he said unto them, Unto what then were ye baptized? And they said, Unto John's baptism [water].

So we see that water baptism did occur because Apollos had not been fully instructed even though something much greater had come to replace the water. Why did this happen?

Acts 21:20:
... Thou seest, brother, how many thousands of Jews there are which believe; and they are all zealous of the law.

The Word in Our Minds

These people believed and therefore were saved; but the revelation had not yet been given explaining the magnitude of the coming of the holy spirit on Pentecost so the believers were still zealous for the law. And one of the requirements of that law was to be water baptized. People are still zealous for the law and, to this day, do not accept that which is addressed *to* them from Romans, Corinthians, Galatians, Ephesians, Philippians, Colossians and Thessalonians. Not once is water baptism ever mentioned in these epistles. Still very few people dare to believe God's Word and act accordingly. Tradition is too comfortable a rut.

To bring further light to the subject, let us look at a verse of Scripture which is often quoted during the ceremony of water baptism.

> Matthew 28:19:
> Go ye therefore, and teach all nations, baptizing them in the name of the Father, and of the Son, and of the Holy Ghost.

This verse clearly states that the apostles were to teach ("make disciples of") all nations. And yet, the Old Testament states that Israel would never be numbered among the nations.* Thus, this command

---

*Numbers 23:9: "... the people shall dwell alone, and shall not be reckoned among the nations."

could only hold true for Gentiles ("nations"). Later in the epistles, written specifically to born-again believers, the Church is "called out" from both Gentiles *and* Jews.* Secondly, the phrase "baptizing them in the name of the Father, and of the Son, and of the Holy Ghost" is never carried out by the apostles or by anyone else in the early Church. Eusebius (340 A.D.), the first great Church historian, quoted from manuscripts which could not have had these words. He quoted Matthew 28:19 eighteen times without ever using these words. Justin Martyr (165 A.D.) and Aphraates of Nisbis (340 A.D.) never quoted these words either. The difficulty is apparent.

Matthew 28:19 was spoken shortly before Jesus ascended into heaven; it gave last minute instructions. Now whatever Jesus said at that time surely would have been important enough for the apostles to remember. Yet in Acts 2:38, the first record after the original outpouring on the day of Pentecost, Peter "baptized in the name of Jesus Christ," not "in the name of the Father, and of the Son, and of the Holy Ghost." If the command in Matthew 28:19 were truly given, then ten days later Peter had already forgotten what Jesus had told him.

---

*Romans 10:12: "For there is no difference between the Jew and the Greek [Gentile]: for the same Lord over all is rich unto all that call upon him."

The Word in Our Minds

In Acts 8:16, "they were baptized in the name of the Lord Jesus." In Acts 10:48, "And he [Peter] commanded them to be baptized in the name of the Lord." And in Acts 19:5, "When they heard *this,* they were baptized in the name of the Lord Jesus." The book of Acts never once mentions the apostle's or anyone else's ever carrying out the command given in Matthew 28:19. From this evidence it is highly unlikely that the words "baptizing them in the name of the Father, and of the Son, and of the Holy Ghost" in Matthew 28:19 were included in the original Word of God, but were added sometime later.

To be baptized in someone's name sets a person apart from the masses. When the children of Israel were baptized "in the cloud and in the sea" (I Corinthians 10:2), they were (1) sanctified, separated out from the Egyptians and (2) were identified in that baptism with Moses. The same pattern can be found today. When you are baptized in the name of Jesus Christ, you are (1) sanctified,* separated out from the unbelievers who are not saved, making you a member of the Church, and you are (2) identified with Christ† and all the authority His Name repre-

*I Corinthians 1:2: "Unto the church of God which is at Corinth, to them that are sanctified in Christ Jesus ...."
Acts 26:18: "To open their eyes, *and* to turn *them* from darkness to light, and *from* the power of Satan unto God, that they may receive forgiveness [remission] of sins, and inheritance among them which are sanctified by faith that is in me."

†Romans 8:17: "And if children, then heirs, heirs of God, and joint-heirs with Christ ...."

Baptism

sents, just as Israel was identified with Moses. So it can be seen that water baptism was indeed instituted by God, but only for Israel and the kingdom, and then for only a limited period of time.

Since the day of Pentecost every person who desires to be born again by God's Spirit must believe on Jesus Christ. At that moment he is given something far greater than the benefits of water baptism: righteousness, justification, sanctification and redemption. To be born again is to have Christ within; He is the hope of glory; He cleanses us from all sin. It's a spiritual baptism.

Since the day of Pentecost, we are indeed free from the law; and part of that law was water baptism. According to Galatians 5:1, we are to "Stand fast therefore in the liberty wherewith Christ hath made us free, and be not entangled again with the yoke of bondage."* There is nothing that can add to our completeness in Him. Jesus Christ paid it all and we are now perfectly equipped in Him for His service, for we are baptized with holy spirit in the name of Jesus Christ.

*"Stand fast" — *stēkō* — used in the 2nd person plural indicates that *you* stand fast, with tenacity.
"Liberty" — *eleutheria* — boldly with a fearless mind.
"Entangled" — *enechō* — be no longer held in.

141

CHAPTER FIFTEEN

Paul's Thorn In The Flesh

Paul's thorn in the flesh has been a thorn in the flesh to more people than almost any other passage in the Word of God. Whenever someone wants to defend his own defenseless theology regarding God's will concerning people's sickness, he invariably points out Paul's "thorn in the flesh."

The first prerequisite in any study that makes for an abundant life is an accurate reading of that which is written. Let us read exactly what is written by Paul.

II Corinthians 12:7–10:
And lest I should be exalted above measure through the abundance of the revelations, there was given to me a thorn in the flesh, the messenger of Satan to buffet me, lest I should be exalted above measure.

For this thing I besought the Lord thrice, that it might depart from me.

> And he said unto me, My grace is sufficient for thee: for my strength is made perfect in weakness. Most gladly therefore will I rather glory in my infirmities, that the power of Christ may rest upon me.

> Therefore I take pleasure in infirmities, in reproaches, in necessities, in persecutions, in distresses for Christ's sake: for when I am weak, then am I strong.

This Word of God has been read thousands upon thousands of times, but many who have looked at it have read something besides the actual words.

The first thing to notice is that nowhere in the entire section does it mention sickness as being the "thorn in the flesh." However, the seventh verse states that this thorn in the flesh was a messenger of Satan. So we know that God did not send it, because had God sent it the verse would read, "a thorn in the flesh the messenger of God to buffet me." But it says, "... a thorn in the flesh, the messenger of Satan ...."

Let us look at the word "messenger." *Angelos* is translated "angel" or "messenger" in the English. The word *angelos* is used 188 times in the Bible: 181 times it is translated "angel"; 7 times it is translated "messenger." II Corinthians 12:7 is one of the seven

144

times the word *angelos* is translated "messenger." The six other times where the word *angelos* is translated "messenger" it always refers to an individual or individuals. Why not here?

Let us go a step further: the key to the true interpretation of the Word of God is always in The Word itself.

II Peter 1:20:
Knowing this first, that no prophecy of the scripture is of any private interpretation.

If no Scripture is of any private interpretation, then I dare not interpret it or you or anyone else. Then how could it possibly be interpreted? The answer is simple; if it is of no private interpretation, then it must of necessity interpret itself. This it does.

The Word of God interprets itself where written or within the context or it has been used elsewhere at some earlier time.

Since the words "thorn in the flesh" in II Corinthians 12:7 are not explained in the verse itself or in the context, it *must* have been used previously in the Bible if the Word of God be true.

In Numbers 33 we note that God instructed Moses

The Word in Our Minds

to speak to the children of Israel and to inform them
regarding the inhabitants of the land into which the
children of Israel were about to enter, that they must
by all means refrain from fraternizing with the
inhabitants. If not, the consequences are told.

> Numbers 33:55:
> ... then it shall come to pass, that those which ye
> let remain of them *shall be* pricks in your eyes,
> and thorns in your sides ....

The people, the inhabitants, would be pricks in the
eyes of the children of Israel and thorns in their sides.
So the "thorn in the flesh" is in this passage definitely and distinctly people. "Thorn in the flesh"
then is not a literal fact; but a figurative truth. It is
similar to our current statement about a man who
would give "the shirt off of his back." We do not
mean that he would literally take his shirt off and
give it away; we mean it to indicate figuratively that
such a man is very good-hearted and generous. Likewise, "the thorn in the flesh," is a figure of speech*
referring to how people hinder or obstruct.

Again in Joshua is another record about "thorns."

Hypocatastasis — Resemblance by implication. One noun is named, the
other implied. It is the superlative degree of resemblance.

Joshua 23:13:

Know for a certainty that the Lord your God
will no more drive out *any of* these nations from
before you; but they shall be snares and traps
unto you, and scourges in your sides, and thorns
in your eyes ....

If you had a thorn in your eye, would you have it
in your flesh? Again this is a figure of speech clearly
indicating people.

Judges 2:3:

... I will not drive them out [referring to inhabitants of the land] from before you; but they
shall be *as thorns* in your sides ....

Again, it is people who are referred to as thorns. A
number of times I have heard people say, "He (or
she) is sure a thorn in the flesh," meaning an
individual was irritating to them. Then why say that
Paul's thorn in the flesh was sickness, bad eyesight or
something else when the Word of God specifically
refers to people as being "thorns in the flesh."

Paul's "thorn in the flesh" was the fighting and
opposition to his ministry by people. They were men
trying to inflict the law of circumcision upon the
Gentile converts and believers. These people were
"messengers of Satan" buffeting the ministry of Paul.

147

The Word in Our Minds

II Corinthians 11:24 says, "... five times received I [Paul] forty *stripes* save one." It takes people to inflict whippings. That would be a "thorn in the flesh." Verses 25 and 26 continue, "Thrice [3 times] was I beaten with rods, once was I stoned ... *in* perils by *mine own* countrymen ... *in* perils among false brethren."

With all this data from the Word of God, without any private interpretation, how can anyone say or contend that Paul's "thorn in the flesh" was sickness? Paul was not sick, He was just sick and tired of the people who were opposing and fighting his ministry, hindering him from doing as much as he would like to do.

These "false brethren" were his "thorn in the flesh" and three times he prayed for their removal but the Lord said to him, "My grace is sufficient for thee: for my strength is made perfect in weakness ...."

A man's true color is quickly seen when he is confronted by his foes. The enemies bring out the true character in a man. So it was with Paul. He did not dare rely upon his own strength, he had to rely upon God's abundant supply. A weak man with God on his side is strong, but a strong man without God is weak.

148

Do not disgrace yourself, God, the Bible or the great Apostle Paul by saying Paul's "thorn in the flesh" was sickness. It was not. It was, is, and ever will be *people,* if the Word of God is true — and true it is.

People say, "Misery seeks company," and when man in his sickness can think of Paul's "thorn in the flesh" as sickness, man seems to get a more comfortable feeling about his own disease, saying, "Well, Paul had a 'thorn in the flesh' so I suppose I can bear my sickness." What a false comfort; what an injustice to God, the Bible and the Apostle Paul.

Paul was "afflicted" not with sickness, but with people hindering his ministry; and the Word of God says that they which walk godly shall suffer persecution.*

Yes, I know what a "thorn in the flesh" is, even as the Apostle Paul knew, and as Martin Luther, John Wesley and others including you, my reader, may have known. The "thorns in the flesh" are people, people who buffet the ministry of the elect of God. But when "I am weak [in myself] then am I strong" in Him. Thank God for His mighty power and good-

*II Timothy 3:12: "Yea, and all that will live godly in Christ Jesus shall suffer persecution."

ness, for in Him we are constant overcomers and in nothing are we defeated. For "I can do all things through Christ which strengtheneth me," yes, even to triumph over all my "thorns in the flesh."

CHAPTER SIXTEEN

When Judas Hanged Himself

The topic of when Judas hanged himself is worthy of research because of the common teaching that Judas hanged himself before Jesus' crucifixion. God's Word teaches that Judas Iscariot not only was alive at the time of the crucifixion, but he saw the resurrected Christ and was also an eyewitness of Christ's ascension.

To understand the accuracy of God's Word regarding the activities of Judas after his betrayal of Jesus, let us begin our research in I Corinthians.

> I Corinthians 15:3–5:
> ... how that Christ died for our sins according to the scriptures;
>
> And that he [Christ] was buried, and that he rose again the third day according to the scriptures:
>
> And that he was seen of Cephas [Peter], then of the twelve.

If the resurrected Christ was seen of the twelve as verse 5 states, then Judas had to be alive during the appearances of Jesus.

Proceeding to search The Word regarding all of Christ's appearances, let us consider the accounts recorded in the Gospels of Luke and John. We need to establish first of all that the accounts in these two Gospels are identical. It is on this occasion which was Jesus' first appearance to His apostles that Jesus showed the apostles His scars. It is inconceivable that Jesus, after He had once shown them His hands, side and feet, would upon another occasion deem it necessary to show them again. The day and the time of that day when this singular event took place is clearly stated. The time of this appearance is the first day of the week, after the resurrection, toward evening.

> John 20:19:
> Then the same day at evening, being the first *day* of the week ....

> Luke 24:1 and 29:
> Now upon the first *day* of the week ....

> ... for it is toward evening, and the day is far spent ....

Luke 24:33 and 36:

And they rose up the same hour, and returned to Jerusalem, and found the eleven gathered together, and them that were with them .

And as they thus spake, Jesus himself stood in the midst of them, and saith unto them, Peace *be* unto you.

There were eleven of the apostles gathered together, and those who were with them, when Jesus stood in the midst of them.

John 20:24 gives the same account only this time the record states the name of the absent disciple.

John 20:24:

But Thomas, one of the twelve, called Didymus, was not with them when Jesus came.

Thomas was absent; the other eleven apostles assembled when Jesus came; thus Judas Iscariot had to have been living and present.

John 20:26 tells us that "... after eight days again his disciples were within ...." These are the same apostles as were gathered at the first appearance in Luke 24.

Luke 24:33:
... the eleven [without Thomas] gathered
together, and them that were with them.

The time that Jesus was seen of the *twelve,* then, is
specifically stated in John 20.

John 20:26:
... again his disciples were within, and Thomas
with them [eleven and Thomas made the count
twelve]: *then* came Jesus, the doors being shut,
and stood in the midst, and said, Peace *be* unto
you.

Jesus came and stood in the midst of the twelve,
confirming the information in I Corinthians.

I Corinthians 15:5:
... he was seen of Cephas, then of the twelve.

Matthew 27 records the events of Judas' life after
he betrayed Jesus.

Matthew 27:5:
And he [Judas Iscariot] cast down the pieces of
silver in the temple, and departed, and went and
hanged himself.

This account does not say that these events
happened in quick succession. This simply sum-

marizes Judas' life. How wonderful the Word of God is and how plain when once we understand it.

Another account also confirms that Judas was alive after the resurrection.

> Acts 1:1,2:
> The former treatise have I made, O Theophilus, of all that Jesus began both to do and teach,
>
> Until the day in which he was taken up, after that he through the Holy Ghost had given commandments unto the apostles whom he had chosen.

Luke 6:13 tells that Jesus had chosen twelve, not eleven, and Acts 1:2 says He gave "commandments unto the apostles whom he had chosen [the twelve].'

> Acts 1:3:
> To whom also he shewed himself alive after his passion by many infallible proofs, being seen of them forty days ....

"To whom" refers back to the apostles (of verse 2) whom He had chosen. To the twelve apostles He showed Himself alive after His passion by many infallible proofs, being seen of them — the twelve apostles — forty days.

The Word in Our Minds

In order to accurately divide The Word on the rest of Acts 1, it is important to establish that eleven of the apostles were Galileans, but the one named Judas Iscariot was a Judean. He was from the town of Kerioth in southern Judea. "Iscariot" is commonly thought to be from the Hebrew *Ish Kerioth*, that is "a man of Kerioth."

The record of Judas from Kerioth is found in two of the oldest codices. We need only Acts 2:7 to prove that the other eleven apostles were Galileans. On the day of Pentecost the multitude at the Temple said, "... Behold, are not all these which speak Galileans?" referring to the eleven apostles (without Judas Iscariot) plus Matthias. Whenever any reference is made to men of Galilee or Galileans, Judas is left out for he was a Judean.

Now, we must continue following the pronouns in the first chapter of Acts very carefully.

> Acts 1:4:
> And, being assembled together with *them*, commanded them [referring back to verse two, apostles whom He had chosen which were twelve] that they [twelve apostles] should not depart from Jerusalem, but wait for the promise of the Father ....

In verse 5, the "ye" refers to the twelve apostles.

156

Verses 5 and 6:
For John truly baptized with water; but ye shall
be baptized with the Holy Ghost not many days
hence.

When they [the twelve] therefore were come
together, they [the twelve] asked of him,
saying, Lord, wilt thou at this time restore again
the kingdom to Israel?

In verse 7 "them" refers to the twelve apostles,
while the "ye" in verse 8 refers to the twelve apostles.

Verses 9 through 11 continue the account.

And when he [Jesus] had spoken these things,
while they [the twelve apostles] beheld, he was
taken up; and a cloud received him out of their
[the twelve apostles'] sight.

And while they [the twelve apostles] looked
stedfastly toward heaven as he went up, behold,
two men stood by them [the twelve apostles] in
white apparel;

Which also said, Ye men of Galilee, why stand
ye gazing up into heaven? ....

In verse eleven the "two men" addressed their

remarks to "men of Galilee," the eleven apostles —
not to Judas, the Judean. Note the *time* of verse ten,
when the two men stood by them (the twelve), and
verse eleven when the two men spoke to men of
Galilee (the eleven).

Judas Iscariot departed the scene at this time.
There is a passing of time between verses ten and
eleven which allows for this departure, so verse eleven
could well begin a new paragraph. Note that verse
eleven does *not* say, "Which also said *unto* them."
Had it read "unto them," the pronoun "them" would
have referred back to the twelve (the same as verse
ten) and this would be inaccurate for the "two men"
spoke to only eleven apostles from Galilee: "Which
also said, Ye men of Galilee ...." This change from
using pronouns through verse ten to "men of Galilee"
in verse eleven is certainly no accident. How wonder-
fully accurate the Word of God is.

Acts 1:12:
Then returned they [the eleven] unto Jerusalem
from the mount called Olivet ....

They, the "men of Galilee" (without Judas, the
Judean) returned unto Jerusalem.

Verse 13:
And when they [the men of Galilee] were come

in, they [eleven apostles] went up into an upper
room, where abode ....

Eleven men of Galilee are then all named one by
one. Judas Iscariot is never heard of again. Peter tells
what happened to Judas in verse 18.

> Acts 1:18:
> Now this man [Judas Iscariot] purchased a field
> with the reward of iniquity; and falling head-
> long, he burst asunder in the midst, and all his
> bowels gushed out.

Choosing a replacement for Judas then followed in
short order. It was very fitting that this should take
place so close to the ascension, and yet before Pentecost. A replacement was not chosen earlier because
Judas was still alive.

Now we have the whole story of Judas Iscariot
who betrayed the Son of God and then regained
apparent fellowship with the other eleven after the
crucifixion for he was with them during Christ's
several appearances. Finally Judas was found at the
scene of the ascension. Afterwards he departed and
hanged himself.

The term "hanged himself" implies to the Western
mind that he took his own life by suspending himself

The Word in Our Minds

from the neck. This however is not the case according to Eastern custom. We read of King Saul falling upon his own sword. This was the method of hanging for government or military personnel. Judas was not in this category. Being a common man, he fell upon a stake. The term "hanging" is used for this type of suicide because the victims suspended themselves on pointed objects. By such action the abdomen was punctured and the bowels gushed out, as is described.

In order to note the so-called discrepancy regarding Judas' death as recorded in Matthew 27:3–10 and Acts 1:15–20, let us note the Word of God accurately and see for ourselves that there is no discrepancy whatsoever in these two accounts.

> Acts 1:15:
> And in those days [the days between the ascension and the day of Pentecost] Peter stood up in the midst of the disciples, and said, (the number of names together were about an hundred and twenty).

Note that this is not the day of Pentecost, but this is in the days before Pentecost. How long before Pentecost we do not know but we do know that it was after the ascension and before the day of Pentecost. On this occasion *before* Pentecost, the names together were *about* one hundred and twenty.

160

It was at this time that Peter stood up among the disciples and led the meeting to elect someone to replace Judas Iscariot who had hanged himself after the ascension.

Verses 16—18:
[Peter said,] Men *and* brethren, this scripture must needs have been fulfilled, which the Holy Ghost by the mouth of David spake before concerning Judas, which was guide to them that took Jesus.

For he was numbered with us, and had obtained part of this ministry.

Now this man purchased a field with the reward of iniquity; and falling headlong, he burst asunder in the midst, and all his bowels gushed out.

The word "purchased" is the word "provided." It is the same word used in Matthew 10:9 where it states, "Provide neither gold ...." Judas purchased or provided for himself "... a field with the reward of iniquity ...." The word "field" in this verse is the Greek word *chōrion* meaning "property." Judas provided for himself a property which he purchased "... with the reward of iniquity." Most people believe that his reward of iniquity was the thirty pieces of silver, which cannot be true because he cast them down in the temple.*

In John 12:6 we are told that Judas "was a thief, and had the bag, and bare what was put therein." Judas was the treasurer or the caretaker of the money of the apostles. It also instructs us that he "was a thief." Judas stole money from the bag, and with this stolen money, which is called the "reward of iniquity," he provided for himself a property.

After the ascension, as we have traced earlier in this study, Judas returned to his own purchased property which he had acquired with money stolen from the bag "... and falling headlong, he burst asunder in the midst, and all his bowels gushed out." It plainly states that he hanged himself on his own property sometime after the ascension and before Pentecost because the "about a hundred and twenty" elected someone to replace Judas, as we noted in verse fifteen, "in those days" before the day of Pentecost.

Acts 1:19:
And it was known unto all the dwellers at Jerusalem; insomuch as that field is called in their proper tongue, Aceldama, that is to say, The field of blood.

*Matthew 27:5: "And he cast down the pieces of silver in the temple, and departed, and went and hanged himself."

Note very carefully that in this verse the property which Judas purchased or provided for himself is called *Aceldama,* the field of blood. It could not have been called "the field of blood" when he purchased it or provided it for himself, but it was called this later because he hanged himself on his own property.

Matthew 27 gives the following account of Judas.

Matthew 27:3—5:
Then Judas, which had betrayed him, when he saw that he was condemned, repented himself, and brought again the thirty pieces of silver to the chief priests and elders,

Saying, I have sinned in that I have betrayed the innocent blood. And they said, What *is that* to us? see thou *to that.*

And he cast down the pieces of silver in the temple, and departed, and went and hanged himself.

People have inferred from verse five that as soon as Judas had cast the thirty pieces of silver back into the temple, he immediately went and hanged himself. This cannot be true as we have seen from our study of the Word of God. Verse five is just a summary of what occurred later; it simply telescopes time.

Verse six of Matthew 27 gives us some interesting information regarding what the chief priests did with the thirty pieces of silver that Judas returned and cast back in the temple.

> Matthew 27:6:
> And the chief priests took the silver pieces, and said, It is not lawful for to put them into the treasury, because it is the price of blood.

The chief priests said that these thirty pieces of silver were "the price of blood," the price of blood that the chief priests had paid Judas to betray the Lord Jesus Christ and to deliver Him to them. After Judas had done this, the priests had Jesus crucified.

> Matthew 27:7:
> And they [the chief priests] took counsel [They got together in a discussion as to what to do with the thirty pieces of silver since it was not lawful for them to be put back into the treasury, because they were the price of blood.], and bought [purchased in the open market place where the sales of properties and fields were made] with them [the thirty pieces of silver] the potter's field, to bury strangers in.

The word "field" in Matthew 27:7 is not the same word *chōrion* as the word "field" in Acts 1:18, which we have discussed. The word "field" in Matthew is the Greek word *agros* meaning a larger area than the *chōrion,* property, purchased by Judas.

The chief priests, after due consideration and counsel, purposely decided to go to the open market and there to buy a potter's field. They did not buy the property on which Judas hanged himself for that was Judas' own property. The chief priests took the thirty pieces of silver and deliberately purchased a field in which to bury strangers — meaning the poor people, criminals and those who had no other place to be buried. This field was called "the potter's field."

Matthew 27:8:
Wherefore that field was called, The field of blood, unto this day.

When the chief priests went to the market place to buy the potter's field, they did not go out to buy a field called "the field of blood"; but it was called thus by the people later because the priests had purchased it with the thirty pieces of silver. The word "field" in this verse, again, is the word *agros* in the Greek, and the word "blood" is the word *haimatos* in the Greek. This is an entirely different field from the one referred to in Acts. In the latter it was a property, and the property was "the property of blood" using the word *Aceldama,* while in Matthew it is called "the field of blood," namely, *agros haimatos.*

Thus, there is no contradiction between the records of Acts and Matthew. As a matter of fact, a very careful study of these facts makes the record detailed and real. It thrills our hearts when we see the great accuracy of the wonderful Word of God.

CHAPTER SEVENTEEN

Study: Be Diligent

In this study we are primarily concerned not with a whole chapter or even a verse of Scripture, but with one specific word. The word examined is from a well-known verse used in the foundational class on Power for Abundant Living.

> II Timothy 2:15:
> Study to shew thyself approved unto God, a workman that needeth not to be ashamed, rightly dividing the word of truth.

The word "study" in the Greek is *spoudason* which can be elucidated and understood vividly by further research. *Spoudason* is a form of the word *spoudazō*. Using *spoudazō* we can trace other related Greek words to determine which are derivitives and which is the root word — the word from which all others are derived. This study demonstrates a basic principle of Biblical Greek research which can lead to greater understanding of the Word of God.

167

Spoudazō, "study," is a derivative of *speudō* which is the root form. Another term for "root word" could be the "least common denominator" — the word in its simplest form, that which is common to all other words derived from it. There is no word from which *speudō* was derived, and therefore it can be considered the least common denominator, the root. Let us first examine all the verses of Scripture where the word *speudō* is used to see the foundation upon which the related words or derivatives are built.

Luke 2:16:
And they came with haste [*speudō*], and found Mary, and Joseph, and the babe lying in a manger.

When the angels informed the shepherds that they should go to Bethlehem, the shepherds didn't let any grass grow under their feet. They went immediately, right away, pronto. Time was involved. That is the essence of the word *speudō*. Time and the brevity of the time involved is emphasized in the usage of *speudō*. To hasten or hurry requires some effort. But the emphasis is on speed or time.

Luke 19:5,6:
And when Jesus came to the place, he looked up [into a tree], and saw him, and said unto him, Zacchaeus, make haste [*speudō*], and come

down; for to day I must abide at thy house.

And he [Zacchaeus] made haste [*speudō*], and came down, and received him [Jesus] joyfully.

Jesus did more than simply tell Zacchaeus to get down from the tree. Jesus told him to act immediately, with speed. And Zacchaeus did just that. He "made haste."

Acts 20:16:
For Paul had determined to sail by Ephesus, because he would not spend the time in Asia: for he hasted [*speudō*], if it were possible for him, to be at Jerusalem the day of Pentecost.

Time was at a premium so "he hasted." He even bypassed Ephesus to save time.

Acts 22:18:
And saw him saying unto me, Make haste [*speudō*], and get thee quickly out of Jerusalem: for they will not receive thy testimony concerning me.

God told Paul to leave Jerusalem immediately. Using the slang words of today God was actually saying, "Hot foot it out of that place! Run like crazy! Move out!"

169

II Peter 3:12:
Looking for and hasting [*speudō*] unto the coming of the day of God, wherein the heavens being on fire shall be dissolved, and the elements shall melt with fervent heat?

This is the last usage of the root word *speudō*. Again the emphasis is on time.

Now let us examine the usages of *spoudazō*, a derivative of *speudō*.

Ephesians 4:3:
Endeavouring [*spoudazō*] to keep the unity of the Spirit in the bond of peace.

I Thessalonians 2:17:
But we, brethren, being taken from you for a short time in presence, not in heart, endeavoured [*spoudazō*] the more abundantly to see your face with great desire.

II Peter 1:15:
Moreover I will endeavour [*spoudazō*] that ye may be able after my decease to have these things always in remembrance.

Each of the above usages of the word *spoudazō* shows the exertion of effort. The emphasis is on the

170

earnest attempt to achieve or accomplish some goal rather than on speed.

II Timothy 4:9,21:
Do thy diligence [*spoudazō*] to come shortly unto me.

Do thy diligence [*spoudazō*] to come before winter ....

Titus 3:12:
When I shall send Artemas unto thee, or Tychicus, be diligent [*spoudazō*] to come unto me to Nicopolis: for I have determined there to winter.

Paul was asking Timothy and Titus to make an earnest attempt, to put forth special effort, to visit him at Nicopolis.

II Peter 1:10:
Wherefore the rather, brethren, give diligence [*spoudazō*] to make your calling and election sure: for if ye do these things, ye shall never fall.

Christians should exert every effort necessary to make their calling and election sure. Effort rather than speed is the prime concern.

171

II Peter 3:14:
Wherefore, beloved, seeing that ye look for such things, be diligent [*spoudazō*] that ye may be found of him in peace, without spot, and blameless.

As you look for this new heaven and earth, be diligent, exert an effort "... that ye may be found of him in peace, without spot, and blameless."

Hebrews 4:11:
Let us labour [*spoudazō*] therefore to enter into that rest, lest any man fall after the same example of unbelief.

Again the word labor, *spoudazō*, means to exert an effort.

Galatians 2:10:
Only *they would* that we should remember the poor; the same which I also was forward [*spoudazō*] to do.

Here the word *spoudazō* is translated "forward." From the other usages already examined it can easily be seen that here, too, the meaning is to exert an effort.

We have taken the word *spoudason* and traced it as

172

a form of *spoudazō* which is a derivative of the word *speudō*. Following through the progression of the meanings of these words, we arrive at a more comprehensive understanding of the word "study" in II Timothy 2:15. It means to "be active" and "watchfully diligent." We could translate it "to be earnest about" or "earnestly diligent." Another good translation would be "striving earnestly." Summing up everything, the depth of the meaning of "study" is to expend a diligent effort remembering the brevity of time. In other words, "Give it everything you've got." God is telling us to exert an effort earnestly and diligently, utilizing our time wisely. The emphasis is on effort, but the root *speudō* brings across the wise use of time. Applying this to the rest of the verse we are to exert the effort to show ourselves approved unto God, rightly dividing the Word of truth. It should be obvious that the only way to rightly divide the Word of God is to study it. Thus we are in reality being told in II Timothy 2:15 to "*study* earnestly, diligently, exerting an effort, utilizing our time wisely." Many people exert an effort, but waste too much time. Others hurry, but exert little effort. We are told to exert the effort and utilize time wisely.

At football games I often marvel at how many touchdowns the players can make in the last two minutes of the game. Theoretically speaking, if they can make that many touchdowns during the last two

173

minutes, they can make that many for sixty minutes if they are geared properly. There must be something the football players do during the last two minutes that they fail to do the other fifty-eight minutes. That something they do is putting forth with diligence and watchfulness extra effort because they know time is running out. This is like the word *spoudason* in II Timothy 2:15, "Study to show thyself approved unto God." How should we study? We study by putting forth the effort diligently and utilizing our time wisely.

. . . .

Other Related Words

> II Corinthians 8:22:
> And we have sent with them our brother, whom we have oftentimes proved diligent [*spoudaios*, adjective] in many things, but now much more diligent [*spoudaios*, the comparative of the adjective], upon the great confidence which *I have* in you.

Paul said one of the brothers whom he sent with Titus had "proved diligent," he had exerted effort for the cause, but now he had put forth even more effort. He had "put his shoulder to the wheel." The time is not emphasized; effort is.

174

Luke 7:4:
And when they came to Jesus, they besought him instantly [*spoudaiōs,* adverb], saying, That he was worthy for whom he should do this.

The word "besought" is a clue to the meaning of *spoudaiōs.* They did more than just ask Jesus. They "besought" Him; they put forth effort. A more accurate translation of *spoudaiōs* would be "diligently." Compare Titus 3:13 and Philippians 2:28 to see that this derivative emphasizes effort rather than time.

Titus 3:13:
Bring Zenas the lawyer and Apollos on their journey diligently [*spoudaiōs,* adverb] that nothing be wanting unto them.

Paul was instructing Titus to bring Zenas and Apollos on their journey. He especially said to put forth some effort for their needs.

Philippians 2:28:
I sent him therefore the more carefully [*spoudaioterōs,* adverb, comparative of *spoudaiōs,* Luke 7:4 and Titus 3:13], that, when ye see him again, ye may rejoice, and that I may be the less sorrowful.

To be careful or watchful of anything requires

effort. The word "diligently" could also be used here accurately.

> Romans 12:8:
> Or he that exhorteth, on exhortation: he that giveth, *let him do it* with simplicity; he that ruleth, with diligence [*spoudē,* noun, dative case] he that sheweth mercy, with cheerfulness.

He that rules is to put forth some effort in his position. It is not just a position of honor. Speed is not emphasized.

> Romans 12:11:
> Not slothful in business [*spoudē,* noun, dative case] ; fervent in spirit; serving the Lord.

The word "slothful" is "wasting time." A more consistent translation of business (*spoudē*) would be "diligence." Do not delay or waste time in putting forth effort in whatever is your function in serving the Lord. The use of the word slothful shows that *spoudē* emphasizes effect. If it emphasized time, "slothful" would be unnecessary. Compare how each derivative fits a specific emphasis consistently, not haphazardly.

> II Corinthians 8:7:
> Therefore, as ye abound in every *thing, in* faith,

and utterance, and knowledge, and *in* all diligence [*spoudē,* noun, dative case], and *in* your
love to us, *see* that ye abound in this grace also.

Paul said the Corinthians abounded in everything
including diligence in their effort for the ministry.
The emphasis is on the effort they put forth.

II Corinthians 7:11,12:
For behold this selfsame thing, that ye sorrowed
after a godly sort, what carefulness [*spoudē,*
noun, accusative case] it wrought in you, yea,
what clearing of yourselves, yea, *what* indignation, yea, *what* fear, yea, *what* vehement
desire, yea, *what* zeal, *what* revenge! In all
things ye have approved yourselves to be clear in
this matter.

Wherefore, though I wrote unto you, *I did it* not
for his cause that had done the wrong, nor for
his cause that suffered wrong, but that our care
[*spoudē,* noun, accusative case] for you in the
sight of God might appear unto you.

II Corinthians 8:16:
But thanks *be* to God, which put the same
earnest care [*spoudē,* noun, accusative case]
into the heart of Titus for you.

Hebrews 6:11:
And we desire that every one of you do shew the same diligence [*spoudē,* noun, accusative case] to the full assurance of hope unto the end.

II Peter 1:5:
And beside this, giving all diligence [*spoudē,* noun, accusative case], add to your faith virtue; and to virtue knowledge.

Jude 3:
Beloved, when I gave all diligence [*spoudē,* noun, accusative case] to write unto you of the common salvation, it was needful for me to write unto you, and exhort *you* that ye should earnestly contend for the faith which was once delivered unto the saints.

The above verses all use the same Greek word in exactly the same form. Though it has been variously translated "carefulness," "care" and "diligence," the emphasis is still on effort put forth. The word "diligence" could have been used in all these verses.

II Corinthians 8:8:
I speak not by commandment, but by occasion of the forwardness [*spoudē,* noun, genitive case] of others, and to prove the sincerity of your love.

178

Paul said, I speak not by commandment, but on account of the speed of others. They haven't wasted any time. Verse 10, "you were willing a year ago, now get on the stick." When *spoudē* is used in the genitive case, the emphasis changes to the brevity of the time involved. The "forwardness" of others is the "speed" or "haste" of others. Compare Mark 6:25 and Luke 1:39 in the genitive case.

Mark 6:25:
And she came in straightway with haste [*spoudē,* noun, genitive case] unto the king, and asked, saying, I will that thou give me by and by [now] in a charger the head of John the Baptist.

Luke 1:39:
And Mary arose in those days, and went into the hill country with haste [*spoudē,* noun, genitive case] , into a city of Juda.

Again the genitive case is used and the emphasis is on speed or brevity of time involved. Notice the word "straightway" in Mark 6:25 which would indicate speed.

This work covers all the references where the root word *speudō* is used and also all of its derivatives.

We now see very clearly that the emphasis of the

179

word "study" in II Timothy 2:15 is on the effort put forth. Time is not to be wasted.

This study is a good example of a type of research that can be done in the Word of God. As many more words are introduced the quest becomes more complicated, but the principle remains the same and can be followed by anyone. This type of research speaks loudly for the depth of the accuracy of the Word of God.

CHAPTER EIGHTEEN

As He Is

In this study of I John, we are going to look at the significance of three words — "as he is" — which are used five times in this epistle. The significance of "as he is" in relation to a believer's potential expresses marvelous truths and thrills our hearts.

"As he is" is found early in I John 1. The first usage is singularly significant for these words are used in their fullest and most inclusive way.

I John 1:5—7:
This then is the message which we have heard of him, and declare unto you, that God is light, and in him is no darkness at all.

If we say that we have fellowship with him, and walk in darkness, we lie, and do not the truth:

But if we walk in the light, as he is [as He is] in the light,* we have fellowship one with another,

---

*"The words "in the" are deleted from the original texts so that it reads, "as he is light."

and the blood of Jesus Christ his Son cleanseth
us from all sin [broken fellowship].

These verses dwell on the topic *fellowship.* To have
fellowship with God, a person must first of all be a
son. A son has fellowship in a family only after he is
born. After being born again, our fellowship with
God is indicated by our walk as Christian believers. If
we walk in the light *as He is* light, we speak the words
He speaks; we believe what He would have us believe;
we act as He would have us act; we declare what He
declares; we are *as He is.*

Comparing the "as he is" of verse 7 with the "he
is" of verse 9 is revealing in the contrast and in the
omission of the word "as."

I John 1:8,9:
If we say that we have no sin [broken fellow-
ship], we deceive ourselves, and the truth is not
in us [in our renewed mind].

If we confess our sins [broken fellowship], he is
[He is] faithful and just to forgive us *our* sins,
and to cleanse us from all unrighteousness.

This verse informs us that God is faithful and just.
Christians are not always faithful and just, but *He is.*
When we are faithful and just we are in fellowship.

182

God is light, so darkness is separation from fellowship with God. It is never the will of the Father that we should be separated in our fellowship with Him. Not God, but the believer breaks fellowship by failing to walk in the light as God is light. This failure to live in fellowship on the part of a believer is sin. But God in His foreknowledge, knowing that man would not always walk in light, provided a way to get back into the light and in fellowship with Him. "If we confess our sins, he is [He is] faithful and just to forgive us *our* sins, and to cleanse us from all [our] unrighteousness." Then, once again we are in the light, we are again in perfect fellowship.

In I John 1:9 the words "he is" are used; in I John 2:6, "as he" should be observed for its significance.

I John 2:6:
He that saith he abideth in him ought himself also so to walk, even as he [as He] walked.

If a believer is abiding in Him, that Christian is walking *as He* walked. Since no one except Jesus ever walked perfectly, The Word encourages us to strive for the perfection of Jesus Christ's walk.

God the Father is light. His Son Jesus Christ was light in this world for He always did the will of the

Father.* Doing the will of God, Jesus walked according to the revealed Word. And since Jesus Christ is in us, the believers, we can walk on The Word as we "ought so to walk, even as he [as He] walked." Look at this significant truth. God is light and God was in Jesus Christ and Christ is in us.

Did Jesus Christ declare that there is no God, that God is dead, that there is no resurrection, no return, that praying is psychologically good for the one praying only, that God cannot deliver, that the Bible is full of myths, interpolations and inaccuracies? Had Jesus stopped living The Word because of what people said, He would not have been our Savior. Had He been swayed by what the neighbors said, by what the community or society said, He never would have walked perfectly in fellowship with His Father. So we should walk, "even as he [as He] walked."

The second usage of the words "as he is" is found in I John 3:2. Let us begin reading with verse 1, noting specifically the love which the Father has showered upon us.

> I John 3:1,2:
> Behold, what manner of love the Father hath
> bestowed upon us, that we should be called the

---

*John 4:34: "Jesus saith unto them, My meat is to do the will of him that sent me, and to finish his work."

sons of God: therefore the world knoweth us not, because it knew him not.

Beloved, now are we the sons of God, and [but] it doth not yet appear what we shall be [in the future]: but we know that, when he shall appear, we shall be like him; for we shall see him as he is [as He is].

When are we the sons of God? *Now.* When we are born again of God's Spirit, we are His sons. Not when we die, not some day, not a "maybe" day, but right now in our day-by-day living we are sons of God. Our life with Him is wonderful now, but it will be even better in the future when we shall see him "as he is." Being sons of God is a guarantee in the present of seeing Him *as He is* at His return.

"As he is" starts with walking in the light and thus having fellowship. Then at Christ's return, we shall be *as He is* and shall see Him *as He is*. This is the completed circle. God is light; He made known Himself, the light, in Christ; we received this light so we are guaranteed at Christ's return to be *as He is*.

I John 3 contains the third usage of the words "as he is."

I John 3:3:
And every man that hath this hope in him

185

purifieth himself, even as he is [as He is] pure.

"This hope" is the hope just spoken of in I John 3:2: "when he shall appear, we shall be like him; for we shall see him as he is [as He is]." The word "hope" is used in the Bible regarding that which is available in the future, while the word "faith" is used regarding that which is available at the present moment. At this moment we have not seen Him *as He is* for His return is yet future. Every man who has this hope, the hope for the return of Christ, the hope to be *as He is*, that believer "purifieth himself, even as he is [as He is] pure."

The usage of the word "pure" is enlightening. The Greek word is *hagnos*, meaning "to keep lustrous" even though living in this present tarnished world. Jesus Christ was in the flesh in this world, but the world was not mixed in Him to the end that He was contaminated. Jesus was in all things tempted like we are, yet without sin.* "Pure," *hagnos*, can be used of Jesus Christ, but never of the purity of God, for God is *katharos*, pure with no foreign mixture of any kind.

We endeavor to make ourselves pure, *hagnizō*, because of Christ's purity in us. Our manifested

---

*Hebrews 4:15: "For we have not an high priest which cannot be touched with the feeling of our infirmities; but was in all points tempted like as *we are, yet* without sin."

purity lies in the renewing of our minds. Having the
hope of Christ's return is the purity in our day-by-day
living before Him.

The fourth reference using "as he is" is four verses
later, also in I John 3.

> I John 3:7:
> Little children, let no man deceive you: he that
> doeth righteousness is righteous, even as he is [as
> He is – God in Christ] righteous.

How righteous was Christ? As righteous as God
because God was in Him.

> II Corinthians 5:19:
> To wit that God was in Christ, reconciling the
> world unto himself, not imputing their tres-
> passes unto them; and hath committed unto us
> the word of reconciliation.

When Christ is in us, then spiritually how righteous
are we? *As He* (God in Christ) *is* righteous.

To be made righteous we must confess with our
mouths the Lord Jesus and believe in the innermost
part of our beings that God raised Christ from the
dead. Then we are righteous "even as he is [as He is]
righteous." Righteousness is from God and has
nothing to do with how we feel; it has everything to

do with God's justification of us in Christ, given to us as a free gift. II Corinthians 5:21 says, "For he hath made him *to be* sin for us, who knew no sin; that we might be made the righteousness of God in him." Righteousness is not of man's works, but of God's grace. No man by his own works could ever make himself even one iota good enough to have the righteousness of God. The righteousness of God to the believer is a gift beyond human comprehension given by a Father who loves us, and not given because we merit or even come close to meriting it.

The fifth and final record of "as he is" is I John 4:17. Since verse 17 begins with a word referring to a previous statement, our understanding is improved by reading the last part of the preceding verse.

> I John 4:16,17:
> ... God is love; and he that dwelleth in love dwelleth in God, and God in him.
>
> Herein is our love made perfect, that we may have boldness in the day of judgment:* because as he is [as He is], so are we in this world.

*The day of judgment is the day in which you and I are now living. This is man's day of judgment; the Lord's day of judgment is still future. I Corinthians 4:3 states, "But with me it is a very small thing that I should be judged of you, or of man's judgment ...." The "judgment" is the word "day." The reason the Greek word was translated "judgment" is that in this day and age, which is man's day, man does the judging.

Our love is made perfect by fellowship ("he that dwelleth in love dwelleth in God") and by sonship ("and God in Him"). Because of our doubly established love, we have boldness in this day of man's judgment. We are not reluctant, hesitant, fearful, hiding our light under a bushel; but we have the boldness to take the greatness of God's Word to a sin-sick and dying people because *as He is,* perfect love, so are we in this world.

Peter and John had this love and boldness for, as recorded in Acts 4, they continued teaching the Word of God while suffering severe persecution.

Acts 4:23—26 and 29:
And being let go, they went to their own company [they went back among the believers], and reported all that the chief priests and elders had said unto them.

And when they [the people of the company of believers] heard that [report], they lifted up their voice to God with one accord, and said, Lord, thou *art* God, which hast made heaven, and earth, and the sea, and all that in them is:

Who by the mouth of thy servant David hast said, Why did the heathen rage, and the people imagine vain things?

189

> The kings of the earth stood up, and the rulers were gathered together against the Lord, and against his Christ.

> And now, Lord, behold their threatenings [this is the first prayer that is recorded in the Christian Church]: and grant unto thy servants, that with all boldness [not hesitancy, reluctance or fear] they may speak thy word.

Speaking the Word of God with all boldness was the very thing that got them into trouble; yet instead of praying, "Lord, take the pressure off," they prayed for more "boldness to speak thy word."

As He is so are we in this world and so we can walk with both power and enthusiasm. We can witness to people. We can help them. We can expect to succeed in business, in shops, factories and farms, in offices and kitchens. Wherever we are, *as He is* so are we. Isn't that tremendous!

Remember Romans 8:37 — "We are more than conquerors" — and John 10:10 — "... I am come that they might have life, and that they might have *it* more abundantly." We do not wait to get power and abundance in the future; we are now *as He is.*

I Corinthians 1:30,31:
But of him [of God] are ye in Christ Jesus, who

190

[Christ Jesus] of God is made unto us wisdom, and righteousness, and sanctification, and redemption.

That, according as it is written, He that glorieth, let him glory in the Lord, [in what the Lord accomplished for us].

If we are going to boast of something, let us not boast about ourselves but about what the Lord did, what He accomplished. *As He is,* so are we in this world. We are *as He is* now, not as He was when He was spit upon, beaten and crucified. We are not as He was in defeat and frustration, but *as He is* in all victory, glory, power and majesty. This is why Ephesians 2:6 and 10 say, "And hath raised *us* up together, and made *us* sit together in heavenly *places* in Christ Jesus ... For we are His workmanship ...."

In Ephesians 1:3 we note, "Blessed *be* the God and Father of our Lord Jesus Christ, who hath blessed [past tense] us with all spiritual blessings in heavenly *places* in Christ." And Colossians 1:13 further edifies us when it says, "Who hath rescued us out from among the exercise or operative influence of darkness (kingdom) and separated us, bringing us as citizens into His kingdom by the work of His dear Son (literal translation according to usage)." In God's sight the believer is already delivered and translated even though he is yet living in this world.

191

Colossians 2:6 says, "As ye have therefore received Christ Jesus the Lord, *so* walk ye in him." *As He is,* so are we in this world. Having received Christ Jesus the Lord we are to walk in Him. We stand fast on The Word and walk "as he walked," and then we are not blown about; we are not tossed around; we are not running from this happening to that happening; we are not listening to different men's opinions and different ideas. We are listening to one thing only and that is God's Word.

> Colossians 2:7 and 10:
> Rooted and built up in him, and stablished in the faith [the family faith], as ye have been taught, abounding therein with thanksgiving.
>
> And ye are complete in him ....

If we lacked anything, would we be complete? No, indeed not. How little of the Word of God we have accepted and lived in our lives. Our level of existence most of the time is far below par compared to what is available in our sonship privileges; for *as He is,* so are we. Few believers are willing to confess what The Word says they are. Hebrews 10:23 reads, "Let us hold fast the profession [confession] of *our* faith without wavering." That means we are to confess with boldness that *as He is,* so are we in this world.

192

To realize the "as he is" greatness of the first epistle of John is almost breath-taking in our day. (1) To "walk in the light as he is light" is the fellowship of power. (2) To be assured in the present that in the not-too-distant future "we shall be like him; for we shall see him as he is," is the fellowship of eternity. (3) Having this hope for Christ's return, we walk uncontaminated, purifying ourselves "even as he is pure." (4) Knowing that righteousness is the believer's cherished possession we refuse to be deceived by any denial to the contrary, but continue manifesting our righteousness even "as he is righteous." (5) Perhaps the most rewarding knowledge is the realization that in this day of man's judgment we have His perfect love. We have the boldness to declare God's Word; we have the power to live a life more than abundant and to be more than a conqueror, because *as He is, so are we* in this world.

About the Author

Victor Paul Wierwille has spent many years searching, and seeking enlightenment on God's Word from men of God scattered across the continent. His academic career after high school continued at the Mission House (Lakeland) College and Seminary, Sheboygan, Wisconsin, where he received his Bachelor of Arts and Bachelor of Divinity degrees. Dr. Wierwille studied at the University of Chicago and at Princeton Theological Seminary where he was awarded the Master of Theology degree in Practical Theology. Later he completed his work for the Doctor of Theology degree.

For sixteen years Dr. Wierwille served as a pastor in northwestern Ohio. During these years he searched the Word of God for keys to powerful victorious living. Dr. Wierwille visited E. Stanley Jones and studied his Ashram program. Such men as Glenn Clark, Rufus Mosley, Starr Daily, Albert Cliffe, Bishop K.C. Pillai and others were guests of Dr. Wierwille's local congregation. Karl Barth of Switzerland was a

195

friend and consultant, as is George M. Lamsa, the Aramaic scholar, as well as other European and Far Eastern scholars. With these men Dr. Wierwille quested for Biblical enlightenment. In 1953 he began teaching classes on Power for Abundant Living. These concentrated sessions are specifically directed to unfold the Word of God as the Will of God and to answer crucial questions regarding the holy spirit and its present availability and efficacy in believers' lives. Leading men and women from all over the world into receiving the more abundant life quickly consumed Dr. Wierwille's full time, so it became necessary for him to resign his local pastorate. Since that time Dr. Wierwille has devoted his entire energy to The Way Biblical Research Center in New Knoxville, Ohio. There, as elsewhere in the United States and foreign countries, he continues to study, write and teach the greatness of God's Word.